America:
song
We sang
without knowing

The Life and Ideas of Meridel LeSueur

by Neala Schleuning
Illustrations by Karen E. McCall

Little Red Hen Press
Mankato, Minnesota

First Edition 1983

America: Song We Sang Without Knowing
The Life and Ideas of Meridel Le Sueur

Illustrations by Karen McCall

Published by: **Little Red Hen Press**
Rt. 2, Box 28
Mankato, MN 56001

Library of Congress Catalog Card Number
83-83093

ISBN 0-9612892-0-1

This book is published in cooperation with Midwest Villages &
Voices—Minneapolis/St. Paul, and Don Olson Distribution (for
trade distribution, send orders to: 1815 E. 35th St., Minneapolis,
MN 55407).

To my sons, Henry and Robert Yount and free women and men everywhere.

Thanks to . . .

Meridel .... *for sharing everything*
Fred Villaume, Jan Eyrich,
  Sharon Dykhoff .... *for editing*
My sons, Henry
  and Rob .... *for going through it with me*
Mulford Sibley, Mary Turpie,
David Noble, Mike Patton,
Toni McNaron .... *for support, advice, and encouragement*
Mary Effertz .... *for her underground typesetting*
Eric Steinmetz .... *for production assistance*
Mary Van Voorhis, Sharon Pierce,
Kris Paulson, Jean Enabnit,
Bridget Stroud, Florence Cobb,
Marion Fogarty .... *for their visions*
. . . and everyone who believed in this work and helped see it through to completion by typing, proofreading, or just supporting me and keeping me sane.

Special thanks to Karen McCall for her inspiring illustrations.

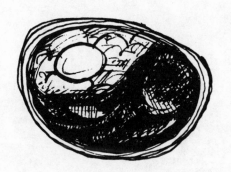

Antoinette Lucy

Marian Wharton
Le Sueur

Meridel and Rachel

Meridel...

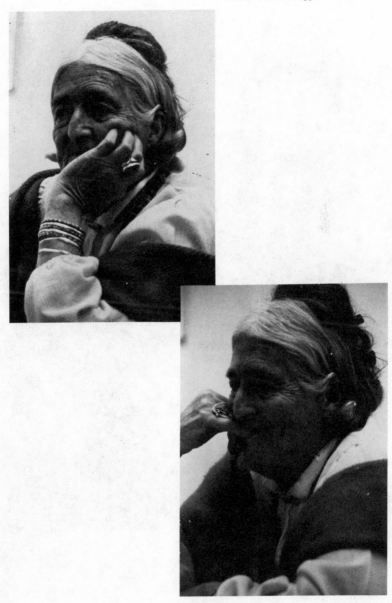

All uncredited photographs are from the private collection of Meridel Le Sueur.

"You Can't Hatch Anything Without Heat"[1]

Once upon a time there was a beautiful lady writer. Her name was Meridel — Meridel Le Sueur, and she lived in the Midwest, near the edge of the great prairie. She was old when I met her and I feared at first that I had come too late. That there wouldn't be enough time to hear everything she had to say. You see, she was a teacher, too. She taught me about America, the people, and myself. She taught me about struggle, because she was a radical, too. And she taught me about the future, because she was a mother, and mothers know about caring for the future.

I was a student at the University when I first met her. I was full of objectivity and analysis. I could do perfect footnotes, and I *knew how to count the number of angels dancing on the head of a pin. Numbers are very important, you know. But when I met her, the numbers didn't seem important anymore. And after a while I got up enough courage to tell her I wanted to write a book about her.*

That was how this book began. Meridel Le Sueur: A woman possessing mythic qualities, a writer of merit, a controversial figure. How romantic it would be to write about her! And then we had our first discussion of the book . . .

Meridel: Well, what are you going to write about me in your book?

Neala: I don't know, I mumbled hesitantly. Maybe we could talk about your philosophy for starters.

M: I don't want to be a philosopher, she said flatly. That's the problem with you intellectuals. You constantly want to analyze. Life's not like that. I'm not like that.

N: But Meridel, I have to organize it somehow!

M: I know, she countered. But you can't do me that way. I'm not something you can categorize, or dissect, or put into chapters.

N: I got more nervous. Well, maybe we could just try. I'd like to write about some of your ideas, analyze your thinking, your philosophy.

M: She frowned. That won't work. Writing isn't like that. Not real writing. You have to be in a wholly different place. Get rid of those dead, lifeless forms! How do they teach you to write? Beginning, middle, end? That's not life. And that's not writing.

N: She's right, I thought. But now what?

I was quiet for a long time. Maybe that professor was right. Maybe I should have written about a dead writer! It was not going to be easy, that was certain. I was beginning to have doubts, and I already knew Meridel was more than a little nervous. I could only imagine her feelings: someone you don't know, peering at you with academic eyes, reducing your life to words on a page. At least dead writers didn't have to suffer that anxiety!

But finally we did begin the task of trying to put her life into words. I decided to take up her challenge: to try to write with heat and passion, to try to be *with* her, to understand her life as it unfolded. As I was writing, I thought of Ruth Benedict's love for Margaret Mead, and Boswell's passion for Jonson's life. I would, during the months of research, fall in love with my subject, and those passions will be obvious to the reader. In addition, I debated long and hard whether to temper my enthusiasm for certain ideas of hers, fearing that my admiration might dilute the power of her words. Worse yet, I feared their validity might be questioned because they were not presented "objectively." I finally decided that to do justice to her life — which was always committed to the collective life, to the idea of relationship — that I would leave it to others to look at her dispassionately. I could only write about her as I knew her. I could only see her with my eyes. This would be a different sort of book.

While I grew to both love and admire Meridel, there were also some painful and frustrating moments for both of us as we worked together. We didn't always agree, and sometimes the disagreements were substantial. I sense for example, that she was uncomfortable with the chapter on her political views. I had given her a label, one that seemed to me to incorporate in the broadest way her views on collective life. She protested not so much the particular label, but the idea of labeling itself. Labels are limited and limiting — we both agreed. But rather than back down from my choice of terms, I tried to insure that the depth and richness of her life and her thinking were illuminated. There were other times when I conceded to her greater wisdom — either as a writer or as the "expert" on her own life!

It was not only Meridel's voice I heard as I was writing this book. As I interviewed family and friends, and read the growing number of commentaries about her life and her ideas, it became clear that in her infinite variety she had generated lively discussion in many worlds. Meridel is a controversial figure, and as the number of studies concerning her grow, I'm sure she will continue to be the focus of heated debates. This is the first full length book focusing specifically on her ideas, and I'm sure that it will generate, in some quarters at least, a certain amount of controversy — especially when we get to her politics. Debate has, and will continue, to go on for decades on the Left as to where she should be placed ideologically. Ever since the Twenties Meridel has come in for criticism (from both the Left and the Right) either for being too "soft" for true communism, or too "red" for true Americans. Meridel herself hasn't helped clarify things because of her dislike for labels and names.

The contemporary Women's Movement, too, has a stake in how Meridel is "interpreted." Many recent reviews of her have likened her to an "earth mother" — heroic, larger than life, everybody's radical grandma. They make a great mistake, I believe by clouding over her toughness, her anger, her sharpness, her incisive analyses. By idealizing her, these critics unwittingly disarm her, take from her the keen penetrating eye which doesn't merely ask for social and political change, but demands it. Other feminist critics are nervous about her inordinate "femininity" — an example is Elaine Hedges' introduction to *Ripening*. She steps cautiously around Meridel's obvious heterosexual passions, taking almost an apologetic tone. Hedges also sidesteps Meridel's Communist Party affiliation with the oblique statement that "she said she was a communist."

Academic critics also approach her cautiously. Meridel is not a systematic philosopher. She does not proceed in what she refers to as the traditional, male-analytical-linear way. She has frustrated many people with her inconsistent, Emerson-

ian way of thinking. But again, like Emerson, Meridel is a
"taster," a "sampler" and a "tryer-on" of ideas. Her thinking
patterns are at times razor-edged with criticism and clarity,
at times fuzzy and seemingly incomprehensible. She will try
an idea on for size, sometimes arguing both sides simultaneously! Of paramount importance to her, however, is the
engagement with ideas, moving them out of the realm of the
abstract into the real and integrating them into a com-
prehensive whole. She reminds us that life is not linear,
progressive or even logical most of the time!

    M: A little gleam came into her eyes. Well, professor, tell
us something. I'm going to call you professor.

*N: Please, Meridel! You're really not making it easy for
me!*

    M: Why that's not true, she said grandly. Why it's really
nice to have an intellectual around. Intellectuals are
important. They have all the answers to all the hard
questions, she concluded with a wide flourish!

*N: You're right, I replied uncomfortably. Sometimes I am
too analytical.*

    M: That's what I call the "fetish of being outside." It
makes a big difference whether you see the world from
"inside" or "outside." It affects how you see history, how
you see time, how you see politics and how you see people.
. . You also have to be equivocal and refuse to make
commitments (FO, 22).

    This is like saying I will fall in love and I will not fall in
love, I will remain outside, cunning, keep my head, etc.
And just as disastrous to any final heat of creation or
action . . . You can't hatch anything without heat.
"Objective" removed "individual" writing at this time
doesn't give birth to anything (FO, 22-23).

N: How can I write about you with "heat"? How would the

University respond to a "passionate" dissertation? Some of my professors are already very dubious. After all, no one has ever written about a living writer before — they say I'll lose my objectivity.

M: I find that a lot of women writing about other women are very objective in their approach. They take the attitude and write about you like a case history or something. I think we don't need that, we need identity *with*. I don't think a woman should interview another woman in an objective, *New Yorker* fashion. You should be looking at another woman *for* something. I don't think we know how to do this — write differently about each other. Maybe you should write entirely differently — how you grew, what did you suffer, what was your oppression. Perhaps circular, going inward and opening up an illumination about a woman. That might be a good way to interview and write about another woman — by loving her (T5).

There is no relationship possible if you are outside. Relationship is like a lodge — all within the cult. You cannot touch a man or woman that is done up, insulated. There is no spark. You must pay tribute to each other, otherwise there is a lurking hatred. Life is for fulfillment of desires down to the deepest and most spiritual . . . Learn how to love without violating the beloved. Penetrate with rays of passion instead of consuming.[2]

A question I'm often asked is why did I write this book, why did I devote two years of my life to studying Meridel Le Sueur? My first response is usually that I "had to" or that "it needed to be done." Meridel is a critic, philosopher, poet, writer, mother, prophet and stateswoman. She is a radical, a feminist. All of these qualities interested me personally. She was a cultural analyst and since my own area of academic training was in American Studies, Meridel seemed to me to be a unique

resource. However critical she may be of "objectivity," she is
certainly a sharp observer and analyst of life around her.
Precisely because she is not objective, she is involved and
engaged with the world at every moment.

There are three strengths she brings to her cultural
analysis: her age, which gives her a long view; her work as a
writer which through its diversity and sheer volume give us a
unique record of the past 50-60 years in American culture; and
finally her personal involvement in the *making* of history,
especially the history of change. Ralph Waldo Emerson once
wrote: "there is no history, there is only biography" —
believing that it is only through understanding the lives of
individuals can we find the ultimate meaning of culture. By
studying the life of Meridel Le Sueur, we have a unique
opportunity to study not only her own life, but the life of
America as she saw it. Not only her own individual biography,
but the biography of a culture. As an unabashed lover of
America, Meridel gives us a unique look at ourselves, a
perspective which I hope will engender debate across the land.

Each of us holds our own vision of what it means to be an
American, and we all have our own particular analysis of what
is right and wrong with America. As the twentieth century
draws to a close, it seems an appropriate time to examine the
American culture, to look at where we've been and where
we're going. I believe there are seven basic myths which
operate in American culture: myths which we must understand and re-evaluate in these changing times. By myth I
mean those collectively held beliefs that are not abstract or
outside of us, but images and ideas which we assume make up
our reality and which underlie our whole world view. They
are: the Myth of Heaven, the Myth of the Machine, the Myth of
Mobility, the Myth of Progress, the Myth of the Individual, the
Myth of Scarcity, and the Myth of Male Supremacy.

The power of these myths, which we ourselves have
created, is seldom debated — and has been since this nation
was born — are the moral questions of whether they are good
or bad myths, and whether they reflect not merely what
America *is*, but what it *should be*. Meridel has been a strong

voice in that debate, and while she does not necessarily refer to these seven myths by the terms I have chosen, she has explored each in detail and over the span of her life has evolved a clear, yet loving critique of our collective experience as Americans. In the paragraphs below, I will briefly outline these seven myths, and how they form our vision of the world.

The Myth of Heaven

Christian thought, particularly that strain developed by St. Augustine of Hippo, is heaven, rather than earth centered. It is important for Americans to understand Augustine, because his ideas were formative in the development of Puritan thought as it came to be practiced in early America.

The most significant impact of Augustine's philosophy was the wide chasm between God and the natural world. In the so-called pagan religions, the earth was seen as God or Earth Mother Goddess. God was *in* the earth. Augustine taught that God made the earth, but was not *in* it. The earth and nature were not to be revered with the same energies as one devoted to an abstract God. Western Christianity is the most anthropocentric — or human centered — religion that the world has ever known. Human beings are placed above all creation and share in great measure God's transcendence of nature. The "real" world is laid up in heaven. Christianity not only established a dualism of humans and nature, but also insisted that it was God's will that people exploit nature for their own ends.

The Myth of the Machine

The Myth of the Machine tells us that there are no limits to what technology can do for us, and the corollary belief that science will save us. We've heard of the perpetual motion machine — a blind optimism that somehow we will invent a machine that will run by itself indefinitely, freeing us from work forever. In our naivete we have allowed the machine of technology to run free into an unknown future — blindly assuming all will work out for the best. Those who question the purposes or consequences of any scientific or technological "advances" are viewed as ignorant, nay sayers and foot draggers.

In addition, the Myth of the Machine has polluted our very way of *thinking*, our way of seeing reality. To begin with, technology encourages an "experimental" attitude toward life. If all of life is an "experiment," then if it doesn't work, try something else. Everything is reduced to ingredients in a laboratory test tube. The experiment is not permanent, there is no commitment to anything, and most of all, no personal involvement. It's "objective."

Technology, or the machine, also leads us to believe that everything ought to run at optimal utilization. Efficient use of time and labor are the essence of the machine. Everyone must work at the same level of efficiency, the same standard — set by the machine.

The technologically motivated ideas of standardization and the interchangeability of parts leads us to relate to people and the earth in the same way: The thing or person has no value in itself, only its applicability to filling in for the machines.

Technology also nourishes a preference for mathematical explanations in all fields. Statistics are important now. They determine reality. Aesthetic or spiritual explanations are given no reality or validity.

Technology also leads us to enthusiastically embrace what we call the notion of "optimal effects." We used to call it "more bang for the buck." But whatever its name, it leads us to believe that results should always be optimal — with little concern to how we got there, just that it "worked."

Finally, the greatest danger from technological thinking is the loss of control over our own lives. Arnold Gehlen (*Man in the Age of Technology*) writes: "If an individual feels that he becomes (justifiably) convinced that the machine can run without him, and he comes into contact with the consequences of his actions only by means of statistics, or graphs, or in the form of a paycheck — then of course his sense of responsibility decreases at the same rate as his feeling of helplessness increases."

The Myth of Mobility

Freedom for Americans is largely interpreted as freedom *from* responsibilities and freedom *to* do whatever we wish. But mostly it means freedom to move. With mobility one is free from all restraints and responsibilities. If it doesn't work out here, "go West, young man" . . . Mobility in the American dream doesn't only mean movement across geographic space. It also signifies social mobility. One can move upward and onward in America. But we never "stay put."

Mircea Eliade makes a distinction between the "sacred" and the "profane." Moving as we do, Americans do not understand the depths of the meaning of place.

The concrete understanding of place as sacred can also be expressed in a commitment to regionalism or celebration in a cultural way of the place in which one lives. Connection to place is not just hugging trees, but building culture. We live in a culture today of the mass market, the mass mind, mass communication, mass taste. We all eat the same junk food, watch the same junk television, buy the same junk commodities. We have to give that all up, to build a culture of sacred place. We have to buy from each other, entertain each other, cook for each other, sew clothes for each other, build for each other. We need to ask *where* was this made? *Who* raised this cow? What does this . . . or that . . . say about my life *here*, in this place?

The Myth of Progress

General Electric has told us for many years, that "progress is our most important product." Progress assumes a line, a straight line, along which we move as a society. Progress also means we have no responsibility to the past, we only need to keep moving forward. Americans have a driving need to see "progress," to see our society bigger and better, richer and newer. We must progress, or we are failures.

The Myth of the Individual

Individualism is perhaps our most sacred American myth. Often we affix the adjective "rugged." The Marlboro man is the classic image of our cultural commitment to freedom of the individual. I am not here speaking against those traits which we associate with individual effort and energy, but with the individualism which suggests that the rest of the world be damned, or that we are isolated and alienated from one another. As Americans we have been taught that the "mass" mind is the only alternative — hence our societal paranoia of communism. As a result, we emphasize individual rights to the detriment of collective responsibilities.

The Myth of Scarcity

Perhaps the most subtle and damaging of our myths, is the Myth of Scarcity. I don't mean material scarcity, or want of things or food, but rather an attitude of what Meridel called "withholding the blossom; letting it sour rather than bloom and be blighted." The Myth of Scarcity tells us that our experiences are narrow and that we can only act within a narrow range of possibilities.

In many ways, it is not a myth. I find young people today —perhaps because of the blandness of our mass media — evincing a poverty of expression and experience both. The other possible source of this blandness is an attitude of being an observer rather than a participant. We allow the "other" to experience for us. We live off canned laughter and "acted" tears. The result is both a narrowing of perception and experience, denying the density, intensity, and diversity of life. A culture of scarcity denies the richness of our own personal, social and environmental world.

The Myth of Male Supremacy

Men, our culture tells us, are better than women. We should (and do) pay them more — even for the same work; men are better leaders and should have the best jobs; women are intellectually inferior, more emotional and not worthy of serious consideration for more "rational" work; and, at this writing, are not even worthy of being considered equal under the law. Like all our myths, it pervades all aspects of our lives: from credit to toys children should play with based upon their sex. At its most insidious level, this myth tells us that men define reality and that women shall merely live in the shadow of this male world.

While these seven myths still shape our world view, they are increasingly being challenged by a growing number of critics. There is an ancient Chinese curse which says: "May you live in interesting times." The word interesting can be read as "changing" and we now live, for better or worse, in a time of great change for our culture. Meridel's life span parallels some of the greatest technological and social upheavals our culture has experienced: the nuclear industry, the miniaturized circuit, the Civil Rights Movement, the Women's Movement, the New Science, and the emerging forces of worldwide pacifism. Each of these events has affected her life, and our lives. Many who have criticized these changes have capitulated in skepticism or despair. But Meridel remained a critic whose prognosis was more positive and life affirming. Instead of skepticism or cynicism, she embraced hope and compassion.

Compassion is a seldom used word in our vocabulary today. Its roots lie in the concepts of piety and shared suffering. The strength of compassion lies in its being a *shared* human experience, a way of connecting us to each other, reaching out over the spaces which separate us. It is this shared, or collective activity that gives Meridel hope. The problems that confound and frustrate us, those that lead to despair or desperation are overcome, she believes, by our collective strength.

For Meridel, change has always been cause for celebration. She offers us a process for learning to integrate change — a new way of seeing, an old way of understanding we may have forgotten. Central to her analysis of life and culture is the necessity for struggle. Struggle is the underlying energy of all life, she believes, and is the catalyst by which individuals and cultures grow and change. Therein lies her wisdom and her message for us: that we move through culture and our own and our nation's history, not blindly, but with a sense of continuity, a sense of ourselves as historic actors, as part of the process, in control of our own individual, and hence collective destinies.

American culture today is in the midst of a great struggle.

The struggle is occurring on all levels in our culture: social, political, interpersonal, secular, religious, economic. Most of us, frankly, are confused as to how to interpret the often conflicting signals we read around us. We peer into each other and the events of life around us to discern a new direction, or to comprehend in some dim way how to be "new" people, to integrate all of these changes.

Meridel, too, has spent a life of struggle, and a life working to find meaning and synthesis from the complexities of life. Her life, this story of her life, can be helpful to us in our own times of conflict or uncertainty. We can learn from her, just as she learned from us. We can seek each other to find ourselves.

This book is not just her story. It is the story of us all — the American people. Throughout her life and writings, we find Meridel returning again and again to the central belief of her philosophy: that we must seek each other to know ourselves. She repeats this theme over and over: Whether she is speaking of collective political action, interpersonal relationships, or her own personal journey through life, nothing is ever seen or known in isolation or separation from other people.

Let us all return. It is the people who give birth to us, to all culture, who by their labors create all material and spiritual values. The source of American culture lies in the historic movement of our people and I return to the people, partisan and alive, with warmth, abundance, excess, confidence, without reservation. Because only they have the future in their hands, only they (DT).

Through her eyes we see our culture in sharp relief — our strengths and weaknesses; our genius and ignorance; our history and our future. She knows us as intimately as we know ourselves and the mirror she holds up for us reflects our image faithfully and clearly. Her personal history spans the rise of industrial capitalism, the most destructive wars humanity have ever known, and the emergence of a new global consciousness. Through her personal biography we trace the struggles of women worldwide to defend their families and communities in a world patriarchy committed to destruction and exploitation, and the struggle of all humankind to achieve its highest visions. In an intimate, personal, human style,

Meridel sings the songs of America, and in the process forms the rhythms of a new, revolutionary world.

ENDNOTES

[1] All chapter titles are from Meridel's poetry or journals. The dialogues or discussions are structured from a variety of sources: published writings, unpublished works, letters, personal conversations, and other oral resources.

[2] Journals. Whenever a reference is made to Meridel's Journals, the reader is to understand that these refer to citations culled from her unpublished personal journals, which number somewhere over 120 volumes. Hereafter references to the journals will be included in the text. A key to all other textual reference can be found in the bibliography at the end of the book.

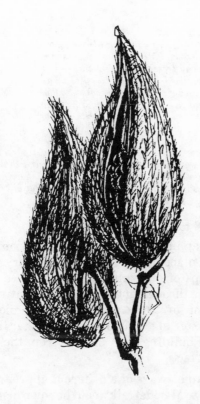

"Send Out A Crier, She Says,
I Want to Talk to the People"

*I first met her at a party. She walked in and she was
pregnant with Rachel, I think. And she was wearing a great
big black cape she had slung over one shoulder. You know, in
those days, pregnant women went and hid in the country.
And here she was, she walked in carrying this golden trea-
sure...I was breathless. It was a fantastic phenomenon to
see. (T17)*

> *There will never be another like her, but we should try to
> understand as much about Meridel and what she stands for
> as possible.* [1]

*I think what is so hard to express is that mystery in things,
in life, which she so embodies. My first remembered direct*

15

experience with her was as a very young child into whose warm life and living room a wild Minnesota thunderstorm blew her one evening. She was dressed in dark clothes —with a black raincoat and accompanied by a large dark German shepherd. She was the essence of mystery — the mystery that binds us to life — and through yesterday to tomorrow. That which awakens us, like a storm, from sleep into living — or a vision of living.[2]

> *The first time I didn't feel like she was larger than life was the night we sat in the back of the car and shared brandy from the same bottle. And I felt, well, hell, if we can drink out of the same bottle, she may be my size after all. (T8)*

Beyond Biography — Patterns of a Culture

Typically, biographies are built on a foundation of facts, figures, people and places. In the stream of history we trace the solitary footsteps of our subject as she moves through crowds and cliques, through meetings and county records. Following the spoor of times and dates, the biographer attempts to fix a person, place historical parameters around a unique personality, building up a picture from the bits and pieces of historical "fact."

I gradually became aware of a different approach to biography as I listened to Meridel talk about her own history. She was right. It was of minimal importance to know that she was in San Francisco from April 14 to October 31, 1927 (to cite an arbitrary date) or to record her social security number. The reality and vitality of historical and biographical moments are painted in different colors for her.

Emerson once wrote in his journals: "There is no history. There is only biography. The attempt to perpetuate, to fix a thought or principle, fails continually. You can only live for yourself; your action is good only whilst it is alive — whilst it is in you."[3] History is a personal record. History as living, history which is seen through the process of an individual's life is never "linear." In many ways, focusing on the *process* of biography is a "woman's" approach to history and people —seeing the events of time and people in terms of personal or familial biographical rhythms; interpreting wars in terms of concern for one's family and children; understanding that economics and inflation influence the price of food; giving a lot of thought to foreign policy when your oldest son turns 18. It is this kind of history that Meridel has recorded and experienced.

The little stories she tells — usually to punctuate a general discussion and bring it into the realm of the real — owe their richness not so much to *her* presence at a particular historical moment but the significance of that moment for the American people in general. Her history is not only her life, but the collective life; her biography the biography of the American people. A close friend once wrote about Meridel's lifelong refusal to see her life as unique and separate from others:

> I have always been struck by the discrepancies between artists and their work. I sometimes wish I hadn't read the biographies of Theodore Dreiser or Sinclair Lewis or Leo Tolstoy. This is where Meridel parts company with most artists. The egocentricity, the pettiness, the conceit and cheapness of so many great writers and artists and actors in the conduct of their lives — they are so seldom equal to the stature of their work. In Meridel there was never a trace of egocentricity. In this she emerges as a collective person ... This was probably true of the whole Algonquin crowd of which Meridel was never a part. Like the God Antaeus, she never lost contact with the earth, her mother.[4]

Or for that matter, her deep love and connection with the Midwest and the American people. In her biography of her parents, *Crusaders*, Meridel would explain and illuminate their personal history in words which are equally applicable to her own history-biography:

> To understand both them and ourselves, the times that begot them must be understood; ... Their greatness lay, as it does in all of us, in the extent that they partook of the destiny and fulfillment of the experience of their nation, fought against its mutilation, embodied in flesh and blood all the agonies, all the lessons, even the fearful errors, all the struggles to conquer reality, all the triumphs and despair of our people across three generations of history ... We must look at our inheritance as both memory and the future, rushing back, demanding action (C, 8-9).

Meridel Le Sueur was born February 22, 1900, the second of four children, her older sibling having died the previous summer. The small white house "with the birthing room on the first floor" stands disconsolately in Murray, Iowa to this day —neglected and aging, its peeling paint and overgrown vegetation a silent tribute to the passage of the years of the twentieth century. Her father, Winston Wharton, was a preacher in Murray. Her mother, Marian, had studied mathematics at Drake University, where they had met and married. But their marriage barely survived the first decade of the new century; Marian decided to leave Winston.

> Then she took one of the leaps of growth for which she was always ready. She welcomed change. She seemed, if she feared it, to always leap that fear and move in new directions. She came to the conclusion entirely outside the experience of her society, that it was a sin to stay with a man you no longer loved (C,44).

Flying in the face of powerful social censorship, both moral and legal, Marian left her husband, kidnapping her own children from their home in San Antonio, Texas, and fled across the border into the "new" state of Oklahoma where her mother lived.

> My mother had to kidnap us. In Texas the women and children were chattel. When we went to Oklahoma my father tried to extradite us. He could send for us just like a slaveholder could send for his runaway slaves. But Oklahoma had more humane laws. The judge allowed me to choose for myself and my brothers who I wanted to stay with. But my father spent a lot of money trying to get us back; and not giving her a divorce, either. He didn't believe in divorce. He couldn't understand why his mare had run away! It was just his attitude. Later, when he was 96 he told me it was because she read books (T13).

Years later, Marian's huband divorced her on grounds of desertion and reading "dangerous literature" (C,45). For Meridel, the lessons of power and oppression were learned early and firsthand. Marian's fearless independence served as a powerful model for the young, sensitive child:

> To those who remember her as an independent, aggressive, bold and brilliant woman it is difficult to understand that for each of these distinctions she had to fight most of society, public opinion and the laws of the land. Women especially would like to believe that her talents were God-given. But it was not so. Her anger, her strength, her determination, even her brilliance, her oratory were things she developed, often alone, and struggled and fought for (C, 39-40).

It is to the women in her radical family that Meridel traces her roots. Her grandmother, Antoinette Lucy, who became an organizer for the Women's Christian Temperence Union (WCTU), along with her mother, made a deep impression on

Meridel. The roots of her own later commitment to radical, social activisim drew deeply on the courage of these women. She recalled her grandmother:

> With her peculiar single courage after going into Oklahoma at the opening of the territory and filing for land, she packed her small bag every week, set out by buckboard, into the miserable mining communities where she met in shacks and white steepled churches the harried, devout, half-maddened women who saw the miserable paychecks go weekly at the corner saloon, and who attempted to stave off poverty and disappearance of their husbands by smashing the saloons...(C,42).

In 1914, Marian went to Ft. Scott, Kansas with her family. She helped found the People's College there with Eugene Debs, Helen Keller, Charles P. Steinmetz, and one Arthur Le Sueur, who was head of the Law Department. Arthur had come from North Dakota where he had, as a lawyer, defended and organized with the I.W.W. and the Non-Partisan League. He served for a time as the first Socialist mayor of Minot. The two Socialists married and embarked on a lifelong commitment to social change.

It was while the Le Sueur's were living in Ft. Scott, that Meridel first came in contact with "political" people and ideas. Alexander Berkman, an anarchist from New York, was a visitor to the college, and spent some time with the Le Sueur family. Though Meridel laughs when she remembers her grandmother refusing to come downstairs while that "radical" man was in the house, her recollections of Berkman are of a warm and sensitive man who spent many hours with the little girl, walking about the small town and talking. He was one of the first people to see her as a whole human being —not just a child — and encouraging her to be herself, respecting her integrity. The integrity of the person — this theme would be echoed in all her writings in years to follow.

After leaving Ft. Scott, the Le Sueurs returned to St. Paul, where Arthur continued his legal defense of radicals and returned to political work with the Non-Partisan League. Meridel recalled the little house on Dayton Avenue:

> It became a center for the early radical struggles. When the First World War came, the Le Sueurs were some of the first in the Midwest to

> speak out against it, splitting the vote of the Socialist Party at their St. Louis convention.
>
> We had a meeting in our wooden house on Dayton, crowded with people sitting on the steps, the floor, to hear the first news of the Russian Revolution. Wilson's ambassador to the Russian front, Lincoln Steffens, told us how the Russians butted their guns to show Wilson they were not for the war. Then Wilson forbade Steffens to speak, confiscating his papers, thinking to silence him. But he went from place to place speaking to these groups, telling us about the first people's revolution.
>
> Rocks were thrown through our window and our books were burned on the front lawn. My mother would not stand up for the national anthem. We were ostracized at school. I quit school as a freshman and never went back (Film, outtakes).[5]

Instead, her mother sent her to McFadden's Physical Culture School in Chicago—a "progressive," open school of the era which concentrated on physical fitness, movement and dance.

In her late teens, Meridel attended the American Academy of Dramatic Art in New York, studying the stage and acting. It was during this period that she lived with Emma Goldman in the Anarchist commune, where she was caught up in the swirl of anti-war struggles and the trials which resulted in the deportation of Goldman, Berkman, and 200 other foreign-born radicals.

Her disappointment with the exploitation of women in the New York theater led her to eventually try Hollywood and the new film industry. Women's roles on Broadway were confined to choruses or blatantly stereotypical roles similar to that which Meridel played in "Leave It To Jane." In Hollywood she picked up bit parts, or worked as an extra. In addition to her sporadic acting in the major studios, Meridel devoted much of her time and energy working with little theater groups in Sacramento and Berkeley and with the Children's Theater. With Yasha Robinoff, she headed up the Little Theater in Sacramento where they struggled to build an alternative to the Broadway style of theater. Just prior to their production of "Blue Bird of Happiness," the two directors were approached by a "committee" of women who strongly encouraged the two to get married! Since the theater had become highly visible, the committee felt that it was time the couple lived in a more "proper" arrangement.

During these years on the West Coast Meridel also wrote

part-time, doing book reviews for the San Francisco *Call*, "so I could eat." She recalls those years on the West Coast with mixed feelings. The true story of those years in Hollywood has yet to be told, she remarked recently. The young actresses kept in "stables" by the studios, the dangers of working as an extra, and the impending economic depression made the years difficult. When she was offered a permanent contract with one studio in exchange for having plastic surgery on her nose, she refused and walked away from acting, turning instead to developing her real love — writing.

> Walking the streets looking for work in San Francisco, I began to write notes, my deepest feelings. I felt that I was not only writing my own deep roots, but the deeper life of all women. This was the beginning of my passional writing. To tell how we suffered, how we were destroyed, macerated, ground out — and my pockets were full of these notes to the world, this cry from the belly (Film, outtakes).

Meridel's career as a Socialist writer began when she was nineteen. By 1924, she was writing regularly for the *Daily Worker*, and in 1927 her first short story was published in the *Dial*. In that same year, after being arrested in a protest march in San Francisco demonstrating against the execution of Sacco and Vanzetti, Meridel made a decision to have a child. Her daughter Rachel was born in 1928, and Deborah less than two years later.

In 1928, just prior to Rachel's birth, Meridel returned to Minnesota to live with her family. It was the beginning of the Depression, there were no jobs. Her husband Yasha was selling eggs to make a little money. The whole family returned home to share what little money they had: her brothers and their wives, Yasha and Meridel, Marian and Arthur.

In the early Thirties, Meridel found a farmhouse to rent cheaply in Lakeland, Minnesota, a small village on the St. Croix River. The Depression was especially hard on a woman who was now raising two children by herself. With many men out of work, women were still one notch lower on the economic scale. Despite the hardship of those years, however, Meridel recalls them with great pleasure:

> In the beginning of the Depression the villages of the middle west were really in bad shape. I took my two children and I rented a house. If you

had any cash, you could almost buy anything in the middle west, or rent anything. I rented a house for $25 a year on the St. Croix.

I'm so happy I took part in that culture of the St. Croix. It was still the old seamen who lived there, the old river men, the old timber workers. People used to come to my house at night and tell me their stories. I was there as a writer and people used to come and say, I've got something to tell you. I'd sit up all night and record the last of the great river workers of the St. Croix.

I didn't really know too much about planting gardens and so on... and didn't get much of a crop — nobody did because there was a drought coming on — but I sold an article to the Woman's Home Companion for $800, and I was the only person in this whole river valley who had any cash... so we would row across (the St. Croix river) from Lakeland to Hudson and I would use my cash to buy flour and coffee, things you can't raise, and then I would give them to the community and they would bake bread, and so that's how we lived. And it was really a wonderful thing... We were part of this wonderful village, drought and decay, and they accepted us, from the city, from the urban population, which I really wasn't from actually. It was the most wonderful period of my life, and to write down all the stories! (Film outtakes)

It was in the Thirties that Meridel began her great outpouring of words. The wound had become a collective one, the blood of workers flowing freely. Literally hundreds of her short stories, newspaper articles, interviews, poems and books stand in vital testimony to her commitment to a new political and cultural reality rising on the political left.

For years the individual took second place to the collective person. There was no picket line, no struggle for civil rights, for labor's rights, for any right, that did not take precedence with her over any longing she may have had to retire in peace to an ivory tower. She was in the thick of all the struggles of her times, sometimes taking cruel and unfair criticism of her work, often disappointed in men and movements, but always in possession of her Center, of her long view of history and events.[6]

Meridel recorded every facet of life during those Depression years in a myriad of journals, newspapers, and little magazines: the *Daily Worker, Partisan Review, New Masses, American Mercury, Pagany, Scribners,* and Jack Conroy's *Anvil,* among others. As the Depression deepened, she became increasingly active politically. Her writings became more militant, reflecting the intense struggles going on around her. She joined the Communist Party, and through the decade, her national reputation grew as a new voice on the Literary Left.

During the Thirties, nearly all American writers were

involved in one way or another in seeking out a new national image. The Depression, union wars with American business, racism — all pointed to a cultural malaise. For Meridel, with both feet firmly planted in the picket line, writing was not the expression of abstract ideology, but of ideology forged in the struggle to get meat on the supper table. Influenced by anarchists, socialists and communists, Meridel's personal political vision would integrate these ideologies into a unique brand of American radicalism. There were people who never read Karl Marx, who knew that the banker was rich and they were poor; and you didn't need to go to college to know who was eating and who wasn't during the bleak years of the Depression. What Meridel recorded was not an imported ideological perspective, but one that emerged from the pain of the mortgage and the suffering on the breadlines.

> I was ahunger and athirst for the being and flesh of my brothers and sisters of a country, a landscape, a relationship, a covenant, a bond. Men and women whose ground had been stolen, carrying on their backs the endless weight of things that do not profit them. Their feet make a deeper pattern in the dust.
> I began to move into the true country and my people. Workers and farmers bore on their bodies the deceit of the oppressors. The dust and contour of the hard land, and the great endless sky. I began to see, I began to write. (Film).

Salute to Spring, a collection of her short stories recalling those politically active years, was published in 1940. In many ways it marked the end of a tumultuous era of strikes, hunger and starvation, and the coming of another war. The Forties found her writing, speaking, and continuing with her political activities. She taught creative writing by correspondence as a source of income. In the early Forties she received a Rocke-feller Historical Research Fellowship to write *North Star Country*—a lyrical "people's" history of the upper Midwest.

There was also another side of Meridel — people who saw her and heard about her as the writer, the public person. In 1944, a story appeared in the St. Paul *Pioneer Press*, profiling the writer "who lived on Ramsey Hill in St. Paul with her two charming little girls." The article referred to Meridel as a "trendsetter," and went on:

The story is that Miss Le Sueur, who was never one to fuss about being fashionable, decided at the last minute to see a play. Looking around for something to wear as a wrap, her eyes caught the colorful design of the cloth, which at that moment was on her table beneath a bowl of daffodils. She snatched it off and wore it. And the brown eyed woman with the strong definite face and finely shaped head was the most interesting looking woman on either side of the footlights that night...

Today she wears talored clothes with big silver earrings and pins for decorative note, but she is quite capable of making a wrap out of a bed spread or hanging and looking well in it.[7]

While we are amused at this society page portrayal of Meridel, the realities of the late Forties and early Fifties sharply conflict with this rather prosaic image of the successful, matronly writer. In response to growing anti-Communism and the destruction of the radical Farmer-Labor party in Minnesota which was coopted by conservative democrats headed by Hubert Humphrey, her creative and political life came under increasing attack and subtle forms of repression. The wave of fanatical hysteria which swept over the country was fanned into flames by Senator McCarthy's accusations and resulted in a reign of terror against the Left.

The Left was forced into an underground existence. Arthur and Marian, hounded out of the Farmer-Labor party, were forced in their old age to run a rooming house to keep body and soul together. Arthur died in 1950, fighting Fascism to the last. Marian continued the family's radical struggle: in her 75th year she ran for the U.S. Senate on a Progressive Party ticket and an anti-Korean War platform.

In 1954, two people important to Meridel died: her mother and her male companion of 25 years, painter Bob Brown. Her correspondence students were hounded by the FBI until one by one they quit in fear; the city hounded her for code violations on the rooming house her parents had left her; and she "couldn't even get a job as a waitress." The title of one of her short stories written in the Fifties, "The Dark of the Time," reflected Meridel's general impressions of the era, and indeed, these were dark years. She was blacklisted, as were many of her contemporaries, and her only outlets for publication were the struggling radical journals like *Masses and Mainstream*. She turned to writing children's books, but here too, she found rabid criticism of her political views. The Milwaukee *Sentinel* referred to her book on Abraham Lincoln as having "pink-tinged" pages. In 1955, she privately printed *Crusaders*, a history/biography of her parents.

With the regeneration of radical political activism world-wide in the Sixties, Meridel once again plunged into the fracas. Traveling extensively about the country by bus, she was participant/witness to the power of people as it burst free again in the Peace Movement and Youth Movement. She was in Mexico for the national railroad strike, and in Mexico City in 1968 when the students were massacred. She was in People's Park in Berkeley and in Haight-Asbury at its height. She was caught up in one of Ken Kesey's parties, and was in Tompkins Square in New York a year later when the counter-culture blossomed there. She participated in both the Peace March and the Poor People's March on Washington, D.C. With the renewal and expansion of the Women's Movement in the late Sixties, Meridel once again found herself the subject of public focus and attention. Her impact on the local political and art culture has been enormous — many groups in Minnesota have been organized as collectives, and most at one time or another have come under her tutelage and support.

Her own work continued, uninterrupted except by her political and cultural work, and in 1980, she was awarded a National Endowment for the Arts Fellowship in Creative Writing, to complete her latest works. Serene despite the flood of renewed recognition, Meridel moves through her days creating, sharing, encouraging others in their personal, political and artistic growth. She is tireless in her working, her traveling, her giving; and her great energies, like a small stone dropped in a still pond will echo for many years to come. Ray Smith writes:

> She's germinal and also she has the rhythms in her writing that you seldom see any more, that come from another time, that come from a deep inward searching and being alone a lot, and the prairies... And in a deep sense, when I think of Meridel I think she has been right... She has that long view. She doesn't think in terms of now or ten years from now. She thinks in terms of centuries. That's why she sees.[8]

ENDNOTES

[1]Gene Bluestein, letter received October 28, 1976.

[2]Shelley Calabrese, letter to Film Collective, received 1975.

[3]Ralph Waldo Emerson, *Selections from Ralph Waldo Emerson*, ed. Stephen B. Whicher (Boston: Houghton Mifflin, 1957), p. 135.

[4]Irene Paull, Letter received 1976.

[5]Twin Cities Women's Film Collective, "My People Are My Home," 16 mm film, 50 minutes, 1976. Future citations will be included in the text as Film, or Film outtakes.

[6]Irene Paull, letter received April 1976.

[7]Katherine Gorman, St. Paul *Pioneer Press*, April 9, 1944, n.p. available.

[8]Ray Smith, quoted in Patricia Hampl, "Meridel Le Sueur: Voice of the Prairie," *MS*, IV, 2 (August 1975), p. 31.

"*I Am A Woman Come to Speak for You.*
"*I Am A Woman Speaking for Us All.*
   This Is a Song for Strength and Power."

*Neala: This is the hardest chapter, Meridel. When I think
about what it means to be a woman there's many things I
feel. Confusion — over how I'm different from men and how
different I am from all the images of woman I've internal-
ized. It's important, too, to know how I'm similar to other
women. I've had children, and I can identify there. But I'm*

27

*also a divorced woman and other women have feared me
and hated me for my single status. I've been poor — like
many women: poor in money, poor in self-esteem, in love.
And I have the fear — the special fear women have — a
kind of vulnerability. And of course the anger and the rage!
Sometimes I feel simple despair — despair over the
damage done to us collectively, to the dreams tarnished
and thwarted. At other times I stand in awe and wonder
over who I've become, the changing, growing me.*

Meridel: Women are all of those things, and I share that
mystery with you and with all women. I seem to be
stymied by a certain swamp in me, a kind of mysticism
that is physical. I do not know if it is organic or part of my
body — part of the body of Iowa, part of the national body.
If it is an illusion, a disease, something I got from my
childhood. Ah, think of it. The spare, the cinch drawn
tighter and tighter, the shadows and laconian embraces
and tempers of those huge and beautiful women above
me. Of those men and the land and the drouths and the
depressions sweeping like hawks' shadows over my head,
over the girl dreaming.

And it is part also of woman. The swamp of subjective-
ness — who knows what is real, what is mirage. Woman.
Girl. A great unknown continent. The great natural
storms of these women, the wind, the stored up whirl-
wind, the anger, and oh, the wound. The great wound
that they were. I am also the wound. The wound, what the
unbearable wound of sex, of lonely parturition and
childbed, the fierce and awful wilderness of this. Who has
known and who can tell? I must write only this. Only this
(Journals).

*N: It's as though to understand America we need to
understand women, and in knowing ourselves, we'll know
our history and our present. It's almost a sense of being
unsettled, of still being in the process of figuring out what
women are.*

M: What we're doing now is bringing the female back

into consciousness. I believe the Western world has injured itself very vitally by cutting out the feminine force, made itself one-dimensional and linear, leaving no dialectic to the erection. We don't have circles any more — our cities are almost unbearable with their straight lines!

N: Bringing back the circular, the feminine consciousness — that's a big task for women.

M: Yes, and it is serious business. Women, you see, are part of the earth. And we have, I think, the wisdom of the earth. Everything is involved. That's why the Indians call it the Mother Earth. They don't mean it in the sense of mother the way we do — that is, giving birth — they mean the profound and absolute womb where everything exists and returns cyclically. (T13).

I the woman was searching. Demeter searching for Being as Woman. Men gave the only orgasms. They ran through you — built a macadam road to go through at high speed and leave. I am crossing over into Woman (Journals).

I Am a Woman

There are hints for us, throughout the histories of a myriad of cultures, of the unique song of Woman. As children, we explore the magical world of goddesses and amazons. Other tales of witches, mysteries of boiling cauldrons and healing herbs, and the magic of the tooth fairy are feminine perceptions and images which lie deep in our cultural consciousness. There are other images, too: the frenzied suffragette, the "Jewish Mother," the *Playboy* centerfold ladies, and of course, the mother-in-law. What is Woman — really?

Being female was, for Meridel, something beyond biology, beyond the limitations of a time and culture which did not honor the feminine. Her search was for the Woman — the woman who understood her sexuality in cultural and political terms. Being a woman, and finding the Woman in herself has been a lifelong process for Meridel. From the well of her experience as a woman she drew the sweetest waters, and this was the center from which she prophesied to America her vision of the circle of unity, a new reality.

In a recent conversation, I pressed Meridel for the particular influences in the evolution of her feminist ideas. She laughed and replied, "I'm a feminist because I have a vagina!" Although we cannot trace her feminism to any particular intellectual current, she has always been woman-identified. Meridel's song of woman began with the humming of women on the prairie. As a small child in Perry, Oklahoma, she recalled escaping the corseted Puritanism of her mother and grandmother and riding off to the "other side of town." There the songs were not the terrible Christian songs to Jesus, but the bawdy singing and dancing of the immigrant, Indian and "hillbilly" women.

> Several years ago, when I went back to Perry, as I entered the town I begin to cry. I began to think of those girls — if it hadn't have been for those girls I probably never would have escaped from the Puritan tradition. I think kinship is people. I loved the farm women and the Indian women because they were so expansive, and I was just like a colt and went and nuzzled them. My mother used to tell me that I'd get a seven year itch — which I did; and lice — which I did! (T13)

Early family influences were equally important in her development as a feminist. Her grandmother was an organizer for the WCTU and her mother was an early speaker on the midwestern Chatauqua circuit — speaking out on birth control and woman suffrage. Meridel has often acknowledged her debt to these "fierce matriarchs," and their blighted lives and personal anguish became part of her reality.

> I crouched below a flock of dead angels who hovered over me. I crouched in the wings of the great female eagles. The angry women, the tempestuous strong and hovering women. Bound to protect you even to your death or theirs.
> It was wonderful. So fierce, so noble, so warm, such titanic and turbulent flesh. They burned, they flowed like a hundred rivers, they screamed in the dark. Their vengeful footsteps in the village. Their skulls and hair and their hard hands. Their fierce embraces that seemed to crush you and terrorize you.
> Nothing soft or lyrical or mid-Victorian about their bodies. They had

the bodies of the fiercest heroines. Of media (sic) of women sent without children into exile, pursued and enslaved. They would sit immobile with their stern strong faces and their high noble heads.

We contain something mythical in the name of women because we always had a consciousness of fight, of struggle (Journals).

This heritage of fierce determination and struggle underscores Meridel's expressions of Woman as Avenger. Their strength — born of anger, of oppression, of the mad songs of their prairie sisters, impressed the young girl indelibly.

In LeSueur's many short stories we hear echoes of the sad, melancholy refrain of her Puritan grandmothers and mothers; the boisterous ringing melodies of the immigrant and Indian women; and the battle cries of the matriarchs defending their families, their souls. The song of American Woman.

I am woman. Grave, serious, mystical. I can't let it be different. After all, I am not a man. I am a woman. I am serious, passional, without much sense of humor. Let it be so. He can be the masculine world. I can't be different. I am dark, passional, myself — and it must be so (Journals).

I am A Woman Come to Speak for You

There is an Earth Mother quality about Meridel and her works that has led many critics to condemn and dismiss her for being a "romantic," and others to acclaim a writer who sings unabashedly the wonder of both woman and the earth. The Earth Mother, of course, in Western thought is the Greek Demeter — or goddess of the harvest and grain in any culture. It is through the voice of Demeter that Meridel speaks to women — and all of humanity. For those unfamiliar with the myth. Meridel has written a delightful 1930s version:

I was telling this story about the man sleeping in the car, and I added this:

After giving him the bottle of brandy, he said: Who are you? I've never had this happen before.

I said: Lay, I will lay you in the fire, in the living fire.

What? he said, Who are you?

I am Demeter, I said.

Well, thank you, Demeter. Where are you going?

*I am looking for my daughter Persephone. Have you seen
     her?*
Persephone who?
Persephone, Miss Persephone. Her father is Jove.
By Jove, I haven't seen her.
She was kidnapped by Pluto and taken to the underworld.
A gangster, huh?
Yeah.
There's an underworld here, he said, lots of racketeers.
This Pluto one the big shot? Never heard of him.
Yes, he's a lord of the underworld.
Like Capone, he says.
Yeah.
And he kidnapped your daughter. Does he want a ransom?
Yes, he wants to keep her six months of the year.
I'll be damned. And let her come home the other?
Yes.
He doesn't want a ransom?
No.
*Well, you'd be his mother-in-law. He wants to marry the
     gal?*
Yeah.
Well, he says, maybe you'll have to let him.
Maybe.
*Well, thanks, Mrs. Demeter. I never met a grandmother
     like you. What did you say about fire?*
*I said: It was damn hot, and the sign above the bank has
     gone off, the damned neon sign.*
*Yeah, he says, it goes off at two sharp. Goodnight
     Mrs. Demeter.*
Goodnight Theseus, I said. Goodnight. (Journals).

Demeter is a universal symbol of abundance and ripeness,
of emptiness and longing for unity, of resolution and synthesis.
As such, it represents one of the most powerful transformation
experiences in Western thought. Demeter has also been a
symbol for the eternal feminine, the Earth Mother who
contains all, and creates all life. A sense of richness and

fullness and complexity is one of the primary characteristics of the feminine, and Meridel expresses it in her Journals in this way: "I don't like blank space. I am Baroque. Like the Mayans. I am too many, many details, many drops of water." The sense of fullness, of containing all, is reflected in many of Meridel's works by her use of the jar or bowl or container as a metaphor for the feminine:

> How good you can feel. A young girl, the jar of the woman. The Indian holding basket and jar. Its great rotundity. If anyone ever finds out what value the empty earth clay dust clod — this is woman. When it is known socially what power this is, what power of vacuum and attraction, to pull in, to mother, to draw in, poultice and draw. Now I contain all this. (Journals)

And in her poem, "Behold This and Always Love It:"

> O my daughters
> My bowl is full of sweet grass,
> I approach in my best buckskin,
> I travel the path of the people
> Behold me!
> . . .
> She moves   she moves   all moves to her
> In the bowl   the basket   the earth bowl
> She is adorned in the middle country
> She appears in the crops of Kansas. (RAR,22)

The container, however, is not static. A parallel theme which energizes Le Sueur's writings, giving a sense of movement and dynamics, is the idea of emergence. The empty seed pod, the bowl, the cocoon — all are symbols of potential for growth and life. The feminine is not passive, but moving always to creation, to emergence.

> If I have anything in me it is yearning. It is the edge of the emerging. It is the full unbroken wave concealing its break with carrying it in. The seed giving over to flesh.
> I will see at last. I will be able to see. It will come through me—not over, around, against, but through. I will emerge whole or not at all. Not in these little pieces, not broken apart like in these flashes, coming out in the fourteen pieces of Osiris. I will emerge (Journals).

In her magnificent story, "Annunciation," a pregnant woman muses to herself about the impending birth of her child, anticipating this emergence:

> How can it be explained? Suddenly many movements are going on

within me, many things are happening, there is an almost unbearable sense of sprouting, of bursting encasements, of moving kernels, expanding flesh. Perhaps it is such an activity that makes a field come alive with millions of sprouting shoots of corn or wheat. Perhaps it is something like that that makes a new world. (A, 83-84).

Emergence is not only individual birth, but birth into relationships and connections and participation with all of reality.

Emergence is a very simple thing. Everyone emerges from someone else. A child emerges from you — like a butterfly from a cocoon — that's what birth is . . . Some whole Indian cultures are based on the butterfly. The Hopi have tremendous butterfly dances and tremendous symbology of the emergence. They call it emergence, it's a whole philosophy of emergence. Everything coming out of everything else (T13).

A tremendous energy characterizes this emergence process; a power which generates a new life force brought into being which is similar, perhaps, to the energy of Spring which Demeter has the power to generate.

Enormous harmony when you see it all. When the pod opens, Beethoven opens. When the pod splits and bursts and releases . . . The body opens, the milk pod. It cracks along the clench, the curve, the vagina, the closed. And you can hear the sound of burstburst. You can hear the sound of emergence (JE,100).

The idea of emergence has a certain necessity about it, that demands a move beyond the initial explosion on to maturity and fulfillment. In a letter written to a close friend, Meridel chastises her hesitancy about accepting a mature feminine role. The woman is clinging to her fading youth, reluctant to grow, and she stubbornly defends the "miserable green girl" who is blighting her growth, retarding her maturing process.

A woman, a beautiful woman of fifty. A woman who has swum the Hellispont. Dared, lived, met giants, wrestled with angels! Good God, a wonderful woman . . . You are fierce, wonderful, lying, often unpleasant, often deeply beautiful — a great female energy out of time. Always roaring and struggling, always shooting the jackpot for life. Good God, you are not this young girl you make out to be, or even this young woman! Who in hell wants to be a green slip of a tree when you are a roaring, multiple-branched, sucking up all nutriment from above and below, tinkling with a thousand lights on a good day's roaring in the night winds, covered with gentle down, stripped for bare winter and grief, twisting, and bowing, showing your survival of hurricanes and all that nature can give. Spew up this young woman, spit out this green mewing kitten . . . nothing will be any good as long as you turn it all back to decay before it has bloomed.

And don't tear up this letter. It applies to me and to all women and it's important we get to the bottom of it. Why doesn't Persephone turn into Demeter? Why are we constipated, stopped up with this young girl sitting in our middles, the miserable green girl clogging our passages? (L).

Growth is central to Meridel's feminism, to her philosophy as a whole. Growth in a spherical way, in a process of maturing and ripening, of becoming, and of completing the cycle from birth and emergence to the future potential of the seed. There is no beginning, no end to this process of growth and circular perpetuation, but a spiraling always into new richness and abundance of self and experience.

In the Demeter myth, there is no death, there is always the re-birth, the coming again of Spring. Traditionally, cyclical views of growth and process suggest a waxing and waning, a birth and death, a planting and harvest. But the real mystery of the Demeter myth is that there is no dualism: only the ongoing process of life generating itself. For Meridel, the circle, or cycle, is a process of constant change and action from many directions. For true potential to be realized, growth must move spirally, interacting and constantly growing through relationship with all the possibilities inherent in the universe. She celebrates the unpredictability of experience, the lack of control over experience, and the changeability and richness of the dynamic flow of life. Growth is not merely a celebration of the end of growth, but rather the celebration of growth which moves through the process of maturity, to the seed, containing the potential to emerge again to a new spiral of life and growth.

I feel I really wanted to ripen. Ripeness is all. Does King Lear say that? Ripeness is all. And ripeness doesn't mean a goal. Ripeness simply means a globular creation and within ripeness is the seed of tomorrow. This circular time of fruition, of fruiting, and not of succeeding, not of winning, not of reaching a target, or not of overcoming the Vietnamese (Film, Outtakes).

I Am a Woman Speaking for Us All

There are two women in the myth of Demeter, and understanding their relationship is central to Meridel's feminism. Persephone is the sparking of change. The "miserable green girl" clogging our passages moves the emerging feminine awareness into a new dimension — the dimension of suffering that the two women share.

In the myth, the abduction and rape of the daughter are violent intrusions on the warmth and abundance of Demeter's circle. Persephone represents an encounter with negative forces, and in Meridel's writings, her "own awful vision of woman denied, occupied, invaded" (Journals) is alternately a cry of despair for the collective suffering of all women, and an angry determination to overcome the negative force. It would be impossible to discuss Meridel's feminism without understanding political overtones of that perspective. The raped, abducted Persephone is only temporarily subjected to the male power. There is sorrow in her plight, but never pity, for the rape of women is an act of power, a political act, and as such, it reflects the universal experience of oppressed women. All oppression, according to Meridel — whether political, sexual, or psychological — is an act of violence, an invasion of the inner feminine domain. To become a woman is to understand the Persephone in us, and to overcome that oppression.

The literary voice which Meridel chose decades ago to narrate the violence done to women is that of the grieving and angry Demeter, not the wronged Persephone. It is a voice of the fierce, protective mother, a mother who understands her daughter's struggles to womanhood. As Meridel has changed, the women in her stories have changed. During her early years, she wrote about the "damaged" women — the old maids, the alienated wives, the lost women. Closed off and blighted, they are somehow poignantly heroic. As she moved into the more political phase of her writings, Meridel's women began to take on more positive characteristics. Their suffering and strength are seen in a global context. They address woman concerns and woman issues: rape, hunger, abortion, sterilization. These women are no longer objects in a male world. Their identification is with the culture and experiences of women: birth, child-raising, nourishing the people of the villages. They fight for themselves and their sisters.

During the Depression, her writing focused on the lives of women, where "survival was a form of resistance" (RAR, Cover). A drought in the midwest drove young women from the farms and small towns into the cities of the northwest where the proliferation of unwed mothers and unwanted children seemed a nightmare. In response to this, the Minnesota Welfare Department instituted a policy of selective sterilization of women — carried out, of course, with the full blessings of the law. The method used to justify these forced sterilizations was a failure to pass an intelligence test — the legal sterilization of "retarded" women was accepted. Those women who had been acculturated to the urban milieu had little trouble qualifying as "intelligent" and therefore, fit parents. Others, particularly the girls from the rural towns, were not so lucky. Many were sent to Faribault to the state hospital, where Meridel recorded their words:

> They keep sayin' I like men but why shouldn't I like men, why shouldn't a girl like a man? But for us girls that work for our livin', we ain't got no right to it . . . They don't want us to have nothin'.
> Now they want to sterilize us so we won't have that.
> They do it all the time and the police follow a girl around and the police women follow you around to see if you're doin' anything and then they nab you up and give you a lot of tests and send you here and do this to you.
> Pete and me sure had a cute kid, but we'll never see it any more. Now I'm locked up here with the feeble-minded (SL, 106).

Le Sueur recorded the culture of poor women — those women subjected to institutional control because they did not have a man for economic support. Then, as today, the niggardly allowances and restrictions on personal possessions created an aura of secrecy and paranoia:

> We've got a radio, that is Belle has got one. You have to keep it hidden because if the relief found out Belle had one we would get cut off so we only take it out at night when it is sure that no case worker is coming around. We had to attach it from the hall which is the one place where there is electric light. We play it long cold winter nights (MWU, 26).

The government was also interested in maintaining moral standards and controlling the women's social lives. Women were followed and spied upon to see if they associated with men.

Anyway, the way it is that they think that all the girls and women on relief is bad, that's the way they figures it. Low grade intelligence, they says... And this woman, I found out later her name was Bradley, would be followin' me like a shadow. It would go to the market, wherever I would go... she would be standin' right over there by a truck, lookin' at me kind of scootched up with a black dress on and her face bright as a clown's (TFG,5).

The girl's visits to a male friend, which she fears will be monitored by Miss Bradley, are curtailed:

I can't even be goin' to Mr. Hess'. Mr. Hess is a very old man. He comes from Virginia. Oncet (sic) he worked on a chain gang in Virginia and oncet he was in prison for a year and it tells on him. He's an old worker. A worker gets old quick. I will get old pretty quick. But he never offered to do anything with me. He's too old. He's forgotten anything about what's between his legs, I guess (TFG, 5).

In a later interview, Miss Bradley accuses her:

She says, as if readin' from the paper, that if you live with a man you ain't married to then you won't get relief, we can't have any immorality around, she says, still studyin' the piece of paper (TFG,6).

The woman defends herself, humiliated and angry, fearful of what is written on the paper. But a remarkable thing happens:

Then the telephone rang and the paper fell on the floor and I picked it up for her and it was a blank sheet of paper. There was nothing on it at all. I looked at her and she looked at me and I knew we were enemies (TFG, 7).

In other stories, too, the Persephone aspect of woman is triumphant as she understands her oppression and exploitation. A woman is sent to Wisconsin for an abortion by her husband. She meets another man on the bus, a Mr. Blue:

I know you, Mr. Blue. My husband, too. You don't care for anything that doesn't touch you on the nerve ends like horse racing, like seeing a horse you bet on come down the course, like seeing the cards lie right, like seeing Dempsey move in with a neat haymaker. What chance has a woman got with this? If the cards lie right, what price a woman? — if the horse flesh comes in pretty and neat, what's the use of a woman? (TH,17).

She gets off the bus, refuses to have the abortion, and leaves with a defiant shout, "The Hell With You, Mr. Blue!"

Men come in for harsh criticism in her stories and her conversations. There is no giving ground to the "predator," the "enemy," the male who represses the vitality of women. Le

Sueur's anger is controlled and directed. Her conversations are sprinkled with the horrors of the many crimes against women — rape, incest, and economic exploitation. She describes herself as a "murdered survivor" — Persephone returned but different. Out of women's trial and encounter with the male, she believes, is born the strength and commitment to the shared culture of women. Turning away from the violence committed against them, women come together in collective strength. Individually, women are raped and abused; collectively, they can create a new world. Persephone returns to Demeter, and Spring returns because of their joy.

This is a Song for Strength and Power

Transcending her wound, Persephone returns from Hades back to life and reunion with Demeter. The circle is closed, the mature woman emerges with a new song:

> Hush, my little grandmother
> I am a woman come to speak for you.
> I am a woman speaking for us all.
> From the tongue of dust and fire
> From the bowl of bitter smoke.
> This is a song for strength and power (RAR, 3).

To be a woman, ultimately, is to be a sister and a feminist. A synthesis of Demeter and Persephone — the earth mother and the oppressed daughter — demands bringing the myth down to real *praxis*, moving beyond the myth to creating a new world.

To be a feminist means to be an activist. No longer are women to be mere passive participants in an abstract mythological process. A collective praxis must be engaged. In order to move beyond the myth, women must join together to counter not only the rapist, but the rape mentality, and the rape politics.

A political interpretation of feminism as a collective experience provides the key to understanding Meridel's "dialectical feminism." For the "female" the thesis of the dialectic is the "male," both individually and collectively — who is seen as her opposition. The antithesis is born at the moment of individual self-awareness of the existence of a difference. Once the dialectic is seen, women who choose to expand their image of themselves as women seek another alternative. For these women, there is a need to define a new reality, a new image of woman and society, through a process of restructuring the realities which have been largely male determined.

In searching for the basic materials, role models, or social processes with which to build the "antithesis" to a strong position, women draw on their own experiences. If women are to be valid in a new world, they must also have been legitimate in the old view. The legitimizing process, however, must come not from the opposition (men), but from within the often hidden, half formed, secret world of other women. Many women's experiences contradict "male" views; if we are told women's bodies are "unclean" we seek to celebrate our biological functions. It is through the development of self-worth with other women that women find support and affirmation of their individual private thoughts and feelings.

How many women created Demeter and Persephone and the exchange of meaning in them? How many? Hundreds of women create the immense consciousness of woman, of earth. Every person is a composite of the archetype—obstructed, or darkened, and being lightened by the cosmic circular around her . . . being changed, mutated by germinal seasons, growths, where the seasonal spurt is enormous and collective. When the corn gathers and appears with all hosannas as a larger cob, when all the collective energies become form and history . . . We are an immense cellular woman, of a gigantic earth and cosmic feminine force.

There is a magnetic field in which we are all living, we owe allegiance to the purity and force of this body. ... The accumulation of this force appears in all and sometimes resonates in all bodies, becomes a huge concept, a germinal knowing, able to continue and pass down in the seed progenitors. It was a long time before this was possible. You did not know your grandmothers, did not know how to pass down the spiral of the genes.

Now this rhythm, resonance, knowledge, vision is becoming visible, known, appearing. So we all appear together and our strength becomes us all, the crop, the highest cob, the seed of the highest consciousness. We are in this period now. This is what is happening. NOW we see each other in each other also — mirrors mirroring, shining — there is no individual in this communal jet. Certain times the entire century gathers into harvest, leaps into form. Not only the bomb but the relative force of magnetism, the love of gravity, — when we all become conscious, rocket to it, then all is illuminated, we illuminate each other (Journals).

In this framework, the true nature of the feminine is revealed — the collective woman reflecting human solidarity. Like any ritual that carries long-lasting meaning in a culture, a mature feminism must capture the collective aspirations and enjoin all women to collective participation. Transformation must be at both the individual and the collective level, for there to be ultimate transformation at the cultural level.

In her only published novel, *The Girl*, Meridel has brilliantly portrayed this new collective woman. Here is a young girl, half-formed but learning. A girl learning quickly from the life around her, a girl growing strong in her struggle toward womanhood. It is from the culture of women that the hungry young girl seeks the way to growth and maturity. Many strands are woven into the emerging tapestry of the woman-to-be; the gossip and advice of her friends and co-workers; her mother's confidences; the realities of poverty and wasted human energy she sees around her; the snoopy bureaucrat.

Stylistically *The Girl* is unique and powerful. The story is not so much a "plot" as it is a pattern — a pattern of change and interaction through which the young girl moves, and by which she is changed and formed. We see her, as she becomes a woman, change through this process of interaction, relationship. Meridel's words and rhythms move us into vibrant awareness of the underlying forces of our collective experiences. She renders in bold strokes not the representation of reality, but the poignant and intense reality of the collective human personality. *The Girl* resonates to more basic rhythms —the movements of love and solidarity.

This collective sense of women is brought to its fullest expression in Meridel's later poetry. In "Doan Ket" (a poem written in the Seventies for the Vietnamese women) Meridel employs metaphors damning the rape and exploitation of women and imperialism and speaks in perhaps her angriest, and at the same time, most hopeful voice:

Down the root of conquest our bodies receive the insult.
Receive a thousand blows, thefts of ovum and child.
Meadows of dead and ruined women. There is no slight death.

After the first death there is no other.
The Body trashed, dies.
There is no abstract death or death at a distance.
Our bodies extend into the body of all.
Every moment is significant in our solidarity.

She continues, enumerating the crimes:

Sisters, the predators plan to live within our bodies.
They plan to wring out of us unpaid labor.
Wrench their wealth from our bodies.
Like the earth they intend to bore inside the woman host,...
They will ground us on the metate, like living corn.
...We are the wine cask struck to the ground, spilled.
We are a great granary of seed smashed, burned.
We are a garroted flight of doves...

Moving beyond the exploitation and rape, at the end of the poem, Meridel closes with the song of the collective strength of women:

Tall and crying out in song we arise
                              in mass meadows.
We will run to the living hills with our seed,
We will redeem all hostages.
We will light the bowl of life. . .
We bring to you our fire
                         We pledge to you our guerilla
fight against the predators of our country.
We come with thunder
                         Lightning on our skin,
Roaring wombs singing
                         Our sisters
                              Singing.
Choruses of millions
                    Singing. (RAR, 51-55)

Once the collective strength of women is understood, there is still one further transformation: from woman to global consciousness and solidarity with others — both male and female. The coming together of women serves two purposes: solidifying the individual personality and encouraging the unity of collectivity. Armed with the support of her sisters, and sensing the possibilities of human collectivity generally, the woman takes her feminist insights and ultimately carries them to encounter with the male world. The encounter, according to Meridel, will be a sparking of mutual energies, a complementary experience celebrating polarities, but not inequalities.

This new synthesis is best understood in Meridel's symbol of the corn. Her choice of this uniquely New World symbol is instructive: it reflects all elements of the life process. In the corn we see the interaction between male and female (thesis-antithesis) and how that polarity is resolved; the spiraling growth pattern of the plant itself (representing that dynamic quality in her philosophy); and the collective heuresis (synthesis) in the fully mature corn, the seed to continue to next cycle. The corn symbolizes the personal transformation of women, the collective experience, and the deeper mystery of woman and the life force itself.

The corn grows, spiraling, up from the earth, from the woman. From the darkness to the light; Persephone returning:

> You do not come from above, you come out conceived in sperm and blood and dark. You come from the woman and from the earth, from below. You come up from below.
> Drawn up. Leaf from root. Everything is drawn UP. If you had this sense instead of that devilish Christian sense that all is from above, given to you by some patriarchal god. Even Michaelangelo's God — holding out his finger to Adam, is puerile. How much of those Christian images in the poetry of Eliot and Pound is so infantile! Without the sexual gut level of the female yin polarity. The synthesis was not entertained (Journals).

From the darkness of the seed, from the earth, and through the corn she enjoins all people to participate in the mystery of the corn.

> Meet me inside the shuck of communal goodness, in the cob congregation of corn. Wrapped in green carbohydrates in ancestral robes we will lie underground in the humus waiting for the enemy together. I have the map for you inside the sheath of pollen, the map to the ovum. Endurance, genetic strength of human, of conception, gunless in the corn . . . Germinal explosions. Come with me. Up the green tidal stem, into the live tassel, leaping from the root to sun.
> Go to the pollen edge — edge of the fire — and the burn. Enter, take off, go. You will be burned into another form. You will break the sheath and let loose the golden edge (Journals).

The litany of the corn continues, the mystery is apprehended:

The mystery is deep. On a hot still day in August the high yellow tassels of the male plume break joyfully in the air and release the golden pollen. Down below the cob, inside the shuck, the bride waits, a silken road issues from each kernel to the outside, the shuck, drawing in the invisible pollen. ...The silken hairs tremble out of the cob of green and moisture. The great female magnetic field draws in the eager pollen. The anthers quicken and burst the golden sheath... Something enters the corn at the moment of fusion of the male and female that is unknown to scientists. From some star, a cosmic quickening, some light, movement-fast chemical that engenders illuminates quickens the conception, lights the fuse (OC,21).

Drawn together into the singular symbol of the corn are the images and conceptions of earth, woman, human sexuality, and the energies of the universe. All time is one time in the corn:

An indefinite presence in the pollinated moment is witness to multiplicity of time and space, announcement from private to multitude, threat to scarcity, pollution, dangerous to criminals and thieves, some message of the proliferation of love, spherical returns of prophetic corn (OC,21).

Through the ritual of the corn we are brought to the "cob congregation of corn," and a collective unity.

In the golden edge of love we are brothers and sisters of the corn. Solidarity of the ovum and pollen, massive fusion and fission more immense than manmade atomic energy. Immense magnetism of the female earth drawing down the lover sun to pollinate to engender amino acid from corn fire, from August wedding, enormous journal of the sun into the small dark ovum of a tiny indentured kernel (OC,21).

The Creative Space of Woman

It is Meridel's sense of herself as a woman which provides the centering energies for her creativity. She gives us a hint of the source of this woman power from which she creates: "The woman unknown to the man always ... her childhood like a deep pool which he harnesses and uses for daily water but whose deep artesian power he never bathes in or knows" (Journals). Through her writing, she invites us to journey with her into that world of woman wonder, terror, joy, and fear, to reclaim what has been stolen from us, to reclaim the artesian depths of ourselves.

Unfortunately, many of Meridel's most powerful passages expressive of her feminine nature are to be found only in her unpublished journals. It was here, in the daily private world of her workbooks, that she struggled to uncover her own masks, masks which obscured her feminine essence. Throughout her journals in this persistent struggle to explore the feminine — not only at the level of symbol, or as a study of cultural mythology, but by tearing it out of the depths of her own being.

One of the most important projections of the Feminine as a totality in Meridel's philosophy is a feeling for the special space of woman:

> The space of woman is different. The inner, the enduring, turning in, wheeling space of earth and woman. The spasm of the ultimate dark womb space — Druid opening. Enfolding, enfolded, inner space, not threatened. You keep going inward, fold upon fold (Journals).

This is space enclosed and contained, yet space which bursts forth with creative potential. The seed pod, the pregnant woman, Demeter, the earth itself — are symbols reflecting this sense of space as potential. Her experience of "inner" is that space in which one centers the universe as a whole, a space which is infinitely expansive. In a passage from her journals, Le Sueur gives us a sense of the power and majesty of that energy.

> The old Indian night comes when the sun and the bargaining cease. The old, old night. The gentle old night I waited for. To cocoon in the seed. Old Iowa night, yes. I waited all the afternoon curled in, waiting, with no cry yet and eyes closed and curled in the woman dark. Woman incoiled in woman incoiled in. And the stillness came and the old Indians came and the still smoke and the still dark and I came out. Under what planets? The planetary belly and breast, the little crevasse. The black head, the woman nut, the woman seed. The great woman mother. The snatching, the passion, the breast of possession, the horizon of flesh. And outside, the earth, horizon of flesh and the cosmic horizon. Circle within circle, all circling (Journals).

We are drawn into this birthing experience, inside yet emerging, experiencing the potential of the seed as it springs to life. Le Sueur sees this inner space, the space of life and emergence, as the ground of all experience and becoming.

> He [the male] was not as secure as the women, who had it IN them. I felt this was a power . . . inner the wheel turned . . . achievement oriented

male linear domains — the space of women is different. The inner, the
enduring, turning in, wheeling space of earth and woman. The deep
spasm of the ultimate dark womb space — Druid opening. Now this is
the inner female wheel. This is the underground wheel, the ecstasy of
the interior. Enfolding enfolded inner space, not threatened. You keep
going inward fold upon fold . . . (Journals).

A clear awareness of this space, the experience of it, is
reflected in Meridel's stylistic forms. The enclosing, involving
and encompassing quality of her style was described by one
critic as akin to the experience of smoking hashish. As any
marijuana smokers surely knows the intense experience of
moving into and an expansion of the ordinary reality is an
experience difficult to articulate, but one which is characterized by a heightening of awareness and a movement with the
flux of experience and perceptions in a unique way. Even her
conscious application of the rules of punctuation in her writing
support that experience of moving continuously through new
realities. She has developed her skill to a high degree — the
long sentences, interspersed with short ones, building blocks
of short, easy to grasp, rich concepts force the reader to
continue moving through the sentences, interweaving concepts and phrases until, at a pause, the reader looks back in
wonder at the distance traversed. The rhythms in her
writings, too, suggest a drawing in and moving through. Her
use of repetition of ideas and phrases, like breathing, set up
paces and rhythms which move the reader into and through
the experience.

The expression of this inner world of woman has often been
criticized as reflecting only the world of "particulars." The
not-so-subtle conclusion is that women cannot produce great
"universal" art, only trivial renderings, bits and pieces of
experiences. Deena Metzger has explored this topic in much
greater detail in an effort to open up new areas off aesthetic
understanding as they relate to sexuality.

Gertrude (Stein) for example, predicates a style upon the immediate
hour, the "continuous present" as she calls it, "using everything and
beginning again." A cycle of repetition, of rhythms, everything told so
completely and so simply that existence emerges as a fact and language
becomes "an entire space always moving not something moving
through a space."[2]

The inclusive, containing space of woman is reflected in the tendency of women to incorporate the particulars into a new understanding of the meaning of the universal. According to Metzger:

> It should by now be abundantly clear that woman's culture, being primarily integrative rather than analytical, offers as rich and deep a universe as that which has been the basis of "civilization" until now... Woman's culture is not a set of rules or restrictions, rather it is a direction, an eye, a broad intellectual framework for discovering form and meaning...[3]

Meridel's greatest strength as a writer lies in acomplishing this synthesis of the particular and the universal. There is a sense of universality that brings with it a consciousness of the multiplicity of our reality, the particulars of which reflect that holism they seek. In Meridel's works the yielding to process, gestation, and the rhythms of her personal experiences are articulated in the form and style which are integrative and synergetic. The organic sense is a particular expression of Woman, she believes. Shut out from the rationalistic, progressive world, women have turned to exploring new modes of expression which are more circular, more expressive of their own inner world.

It is difficult today to understand the terrible struggle of a woman writer of six decades ago to be heard in her true voice, to write courageously of her own experiences and the experiences of other women. All her life, Meridel has felt the pressures on women artists:

> I really feel that women, writers, cultural workers, artists have been subject to tremendous attacks upon them. It was a great struggle to be an artist — and not just an artist. I wanted to be a sexual person, a mother, a wife, and part of a commune or social group of some kind. Of a group of struggling, rebellious people. We all want to be part of a struggle. Even a crazy person is probably crazy because he hasn't been able to be part of a communality. But I think in all those aspirations I was hunted and struck down and shot at (Film, outtakes).

Women, and Meridel is no exception, seem to understand this feeling of vulnerability and sensitivity which characterizes exploited and oppressed groups generally. For Meridel, it was doubly difficult to remain centered in her work. She was criticized for her political views on the one hand, and rejected by editors who saw no merit in "woman's" stories of childbirth, on the other.

> I really was attacked as a woman writer. Not just nicely, or that I was a poor writer. The only virtue that I really see in my life was the fact that I kept on with my creative life. And it wasn't ambition. I never expected to be a great writer. I just wanted to be a writer saying what was true. I just wanted to write what I knew ... In love or despair — I wrote (Film, outtakes).

Commitment and dedication to her work continues to this day. I remember going out to her house to study in her library. In that fantastic corner of the basement, surrounded by row upon row of books stacked to the ceiling, others shoved in between, baskets of newspaper clippings — in the quiet of this place of knowledge, I would go through pages of old words. Often, Meridel would be working in her room, the door closed. Occasionally the tap-tap-tap of her typewriter would intrude on my quiet studies. She did, and still does, work eight hours a day at her trade. Her energy is amazing, but even more impressive is her discipline and the passionate intensity of her commitment to creative expression.

> Falling in love was great, sex was great, I liked the feeling of it all. And I liked the feeling of writing something every day. It was just part of the whole thing for me. I think it's very important to convey that to women — that they have to do their own work, no matter how busy they are. You do your own work, goddamn it, whatever it is! (T8).

> It is wonderful to leave the hieroglyph to be read by someone later in another time. Somehow time itself makes them decipherable. I hope some lover of the future can decipher me. I truly want to leave a message on the wall. A hieroglyph — a glyph — wonderful word, glyph, like the beast that I am, the woman beast (Journals).

ENDNOTES

Patricia Kirkpatrick, "Meridel Le Sueur: In the Cycle of Root & Bloom," *Minnesota Daily* (November 19, 1974) p. 9, passim.

[2]Metzger, Deena, "In Her Image," *Heresies*, 1, 2, May 1977, p. 4.

[3]Ibid, p. 11.

"Do Not Plow My Flesh Any More; Do Not Impregnate Me Without Intention and Love"

America and the Land

Beginning with the earliest travel accounts and handbills encouraging emigration to the new country, the European mind was captivated with the idea of the vast, relatively unpopulated land space of America. A Garden of the World inhabited by the Noble Savage inspired an entire continent to initiate one of the greatest migrations in history, the settling of a new country.

49

In the myths and legends, hopes and dreams of our European ancestors lie the seeds of our modern consciousness of the land. Perry Miller, a 20th century American historian, has suggested that the relationship of the American people to the land is the key to understanding the American character. The relationship of humanity with nature has always been of primary concern throughout the histories of all cultures, but the encounter with the North American continent was unique in the history of the world.

We often overlook the fact, however, that along with their fine, high hopes and ideals, our ancestors brought with them cultural baggage that included a fair share and more of prejudices, ignorance, greed and a lust for power that was set free of institutional restraints in the vast continent. Some came fleeing oppression and exploitation, only to oppress and exploit in the new land. A few, armed with skills of oppression and exploitation merely transferred their policies to the new land. Blacks, kidnapped from Africa to work the new land, and Indians, dispossessed of their land, were the victims of this new migration. But white males, it was assumed (even with seven years of indentured service to complete) could own a piece of the new heaven. People came for the land.

The European response to the land was influenced by a welter of conflicting European perceptions which contrasted with the Indian perceptions of the land; most often motivated by political and economic imperialism (and expressed in broken treaties); idealized in story, song and myth down to our present time. With an unusual degree of self-conscious aware-ness of the significance of the land space, Americans have carefully recorded and analyzed their own experience with the land.

How Have We Looked at the Land?

The experience of the land is essentially a religious one. How space is transformed to sacred place by a culture is primarily a religious process. Transformation mysteries are basic to all religions, but how these mysteries explain the reality of the land and nature can differ widely. The religion most influential in American perceptions of the land is, of course, Christianity — and more specifically, the Protestant sects.

Heavily influenced by Augustinianism, Protestant thought makes a clear separation between mind and body and earth and heaven. For the Puritan, transformation and spiritual regeneration came not from a right association with the earth, but from a right attitude toward heaven. It was not the present which was important but the future. Christianity was, at best, indifferent to nature; at worst, hostile to it. The chosen land was never considered a sacred space in its own right as a source of spiritual energy, but as a land to be transformed and changed to a Christian space which bore little identity with the real earth or landscape. Even the admonition, "Consider the lilies . . ." saw nature as "outside" of man — something useful and instructive, but hardly something to embrace. Sacred space, therefore, was not in nature. It was instead an intensely individual and personal domain. As an inner, subjective, closed off space, known only to God and the individual, it bore no relation to the external reality of the land.

The Puritans experienced two conflicting perceptions of the natural world: one, that America was a garden, a pristine wilderness space in which humanity and Christianity could blossom and secondly, that the wilderness was evil and inhabited by the devil in the person of the Indian and nature was a threat to salvation — full of evils and temptations to be overcome and conquered. Nature was both a place of regeneration and the source of sin and evil.

Nowhere in the Puritan mind, however, do we find a commitment to relationship with the land. It was outside of man, either serving to regenerate his lost soul or tempting him to ultimate evils. This ambiguity also has its modern counterparts: the "Back to the Land" movement representing the regenerative qualities of nature, and our concern with a possible backlash from nature due to our scientific meddling, representing the view of nature as evil and the source of "sin" against man.[1]

By the nineteenth century the image of the wilderness had been transformed. The natural world no longer threatened the community — it could be transformed by moving across it, dominating it. Man was able to conquer distance and time. With the rise of industrialism, nature was no longer to be feared. It was accessible to man's understanding and subjugation. He could idealize nature now, because he no longer felt that his spirituality (however tenuous) was linked to the wilderness. Man could make his own scientific salvation now.

Three myths dominated the nineteenth century response to the land:

> In America the metaphors of nature tend to follow three distinct directions. The rugged-individualist theme, in an existentialist mode, rejects the reality of society. The yeoman-equality theme views homogeneous conformity as the appropriate solution; society is the only reality. For the Transcendentalists, the only reality is that society is part of nature and must build its unity accordingly.[2]

When Americans struggle with the question of nature, they come down in favor of either the rugged-individual theme or the yeoman-equality theme: the one rejecting society, the other the individual. In both, however, nature is subject to either man or society. Both see man as dominant, whether through his actions individually or with others in society.

In *Virgin Land*, Henry Nash Smith first traced the development of these two American myths of the land. In the rugged-individual myth, the frontiersman was symbolic of the American view of the land as an object to be conquered. Nash sees the movement westward as symbolic of this individual's activities. Concurrent with this attitude was the idea of Manifest Destiny — freedom was a function of "progress" and the steady movement linearly to the West was done in the name of dominion over the land and the peoples who had inhabited the land for centuries. Just as the relationship with the land changed in the nineteenth century, so too did the method of dealing with the Indians. The Red Devil was no longer to be feared or converted. He was to be destroyed in the name of progress and civilization.

The Puritan abstract relationship with the land was easily transformed and readily compatible with the nineteenth century emphasis on progress. The land was an object, it was to be exploited. It was also subject to transformation by individual efforts. Salvation for the Puritans had been an intensely personal experience, and in like manner, the subduing of the land was also intensely personal. And since land was an object, it was also subject to ownership by the individual who tamed and subdued it. Intense, in-depth experiences with the land were not conceived.

A second myth which Smith postulates is the yeoman farmer symbol. Hard on the heels of the individual frontiersman was the sturdy American peasant who would people the land and plow the prairies, spreading his village society across the continent. Bringing democracy with him in his wagonful of children, the yeoman farmer was to take on mythic dimensions with decidedly political overtones. He would bring civilization to the wilderness — building his churches as he came. Although the yeoman farmer was much more "social" in his world view, his relationship with the land bore remarkable similarity to that of the frontiersman. He sought to subdue the land, as had the Pathfinder. The Indians were no longer a threat, but the land, as Rolvaag has so brilliantly shown us, was his enemy, and must come under the plow and the dominion of Man.

Each of these historical relationships with the land may express various ingredients in the make-up of the American psyche, but they each fall short of encompassing both a political and a moral understanding of the land and nature as a whole. They give us a sense of where we have been, and in many ways, where we still are in our attitudes toward nature. In our modern ideas of conservation, for example, we still view wilderness as heaven: nature is something to be preserved because it is pure — the Virgin Land. The crude frontiersman is alive and well in our cowboy movies, and the little house on the prairie recalls in a charming way the yeoman farmer.

These perspectives do have a common base: each sees

nature as external and abstract, subject either to an abstract God or to the man/society expanding across a continent — building civilization and subduing the land as he goes. None of these perspectives, however, explore the kinds and qualities of relationship with the land which may have actually taken place. Living as we do, with these myths of the land, the roots of a great love for the land are denied. In a real relationship, we would need to touch and feel and see nature in a different, intimate way.

In the writings of the Transcendentalists we find a more hopeful alternative view of the relationship of man to nature. Emerson, Thoreau and Whitman, for example, recorded their delight in the rediscovery of nature as an equal partner in the rush of building the new white civilization. The Red Devils had been beaten off by the time of the Transcendentalists, and while there would be a "final solution" to the Indian problem late in the nineteenth century, the destruction of Indian culture and the near-genocide of the people would come in the name of progress. The imagery of the Noble Savage returned to the literature, and along with it an image of a benign regenerative power in the land.

This benevolent nature of the Transcendentalists would, of course, be subservient to mankind. Even Emerson, who contributed the most original thought on nature was, in his essay "Nature," ambivalent about his feelings toward the land. He alternately argued that nature had a force and spirit of her own and that she was submissive to the expansive dreams of humanity. Emerson would, in turn, influence the poet Walt Whitman, who sang the song of nature loudly and boisterously. Nature for Whitman had a new role: as the handmaiden of American democracy:

> I conceive of no flourishing and heroic elements of Democracy in the United States, or of Democracy maintaining itself at all, without the Nature-element forming a main part — to be its health-element and beauty-element — to really underlie the whole politics, sanity, religion, and art of the New World.[3]

Transcendentalism articulated an American consciousness that saw nature embodying sacred or spiritual qualities.

In marked contrast to more materialistic notions of the later scientific revolution, Transcendentalism evoked a reverent feeling toward the land — a reverence which overcame the Puritan fear of the land, and a reverence which brought God into a more material realm. In recent years, Transcendental thought has been revived in ecological thinking. Romantic movements throughout history have always been committed to organic views of nature which celebrate the sense of connection and participation and dialectical interaction between humanity and Nature. Modern advocates of no-growth economics, environmental protection and a non-nuclear world argue that the philosophical and real separation of man from nature can no longer be tolerated. Spaceship Earth must be seen and understood in its global aspects — the interrelationships of man to man, culture to culture, and mostly man to the earth which nurtures him.

At a time when Western culture is undergoing a vast re-evaluation of its basic philosophical ideas, it is no accident that the land should also be subject to new understanding. The song we sang without knowing is not necessarily "new," however. The rhythms of a right relationship with nature run back into our Western heritage to the Middle Ages, and new voices have taken up this old song of love for the earth.

Meridel's Perception of the Land

Meridel has taken up this long suppressed song of the American land. It is a song of anguish and anger, of rape and degradation, of love and joy. It is a song that tears away the romantic imagery and lets us see the land once more as the source of all life, rather than as a source of coal and energy to be ground up in the fires of capitalism. It is the land that becomes the sensuous body of woman. With the voice of Demeter crying for the return of her daughter, Meridel wails for the lost and raped land, the earth of fertility and regeneration. She calls for a new attitude, a new love, a new relationship with the land.

You have had your flesh of us

```
Turned to your plow
        summer bright
    and upbloomed dust.
O conqueror, give up the stolen deed
Clear and fall ripe in
        your own harvest.
Be wild sumac, tasseled corn
            and love,
And I will warm your feet
        between my breasts.
I am field of long ago
    plowed and forgotten
And I come to walk among you
    planting abundant corn. (RAR, p. 11).
```

The warm loving voice, however, can quickly turn to angry denunciation of the exploiters of the earth. Anger and revenge are also echoes of the song of the earth:

> The earth is not feeble or submitting to rape. It has its directions and responsibility militant being taken away its yield and its love. The mother is also fierce devourer and defender. Did you expect to do whatever you wanted with no response from the female? She is fierce. The plunderers of nightingales and violets are brought to trial. All returns in the season. We return with the season. What you do in winter comes out in summer (Journals).

Meridel's passions for the variety and vitality of life expand to incorporate the earth herself. This is not the land cut up and bisected by the square, but the great round circle of the feminine prairie. It is an old view of nature, one celebrating connection with all of reality. Rejecting the picture postcard view of the land, Meridel returns to the ancient view of nature as *physis*. To the Greeks, nature was not something segregated, outside, or objectified, but the All, the Everything, the basic stuff of reality. This is a revolutionary perspective, both politically and philosophically, and as such, it has profound implications for the American culture.

> You have to understand that her view of the land is revolutionary. It's "revolutionary" but not unique. It challenges how we see the land and the concept of private property. Do we really believe that we can buy a piece of space, and then have a piece of paper that describes that space? It's impossible. And there are other cultures who see the way she does — that the land belongs to all, it is our Mother.[4]

Understanding the land as Mother requires setting aside

traditional images in Western culture of "mother." In Le Sueur's works we find emerging a new synthesis of Mother —the integration of American Indian religion and philosophy with her feminism. To understand this new image of the earth, we need to understand women and cultures alien to our own. In fusing the essential poetic imagery of these two worlds —the Indian and the feminine — Meridel has brought us full circle.

Americans have never been comfortable with Indian culture. In recent years, however, the "study" of Indians has become popular. Whether it comes from a sense of guilt for what we did to these people, or because of the barrenness and neutrality of our own cultural symbols, the preoccupation with Indian religions and Indian consciousness has become a popular activity. The depth of meaning, however, still remains elusive to the white American mind — especially when it comes to understanding how the Indian philosophies see the land. Our passion for things "Indian" has become a new version of our own myth of manifest destiny. Where we once sought regeneration in the wilderness, we now seek it in another culture's experiences and visions.

> The attitude of North Americans to the Indian world is part of their attitude to nature: they don't see it as a reality to be fused with, but to be dominated. The destruction of the native world foreshadowed their assault on nature. North American civilization has set out to dominate, tame, and make use of nature exactly as a race of people are conquered. In a way they have treated the natural world as an enemy.[5]

In sharp contrast, however, we find the works of Meridel as they approach the Indian cultures with deep love and respect. Her approach to the Indian cultures is partly a re-searching and finding her own roots (Iroquois) and partly seeking an alternative to the WASP values of white America. Her use of long-buried symbols of a feminine earth, awakened and transformed in a synthesis with Indian symbol-making processes, is fused with the imagery of a white, Midwestern culture.

> The upper and lower crossings... the land becomes Indian. He sees it differently. He is not trying to own it, or cultivate it, receive from it something, steal from woman and land. He sees it burning. It moves

into him, he moves into it. He has a terrible dream of old crossings and battlefields. His European life falls away from him (Journals).

She delights with sharing this marvelous relationship with the land, honoring the Indian vision:

Traveling, moving, blowing across the vast American sky. How good you can feel on any journey alone in America. The Indians have left rope ladders down out of the sky and up from the earth where you can climb and swing and love enters you from the movement, from the speed, from the long celebration of the true mother, the earth. The Indians loved her and honored her as she lies there looking into train and bus windows at you — *with* you, never *at* you. Without the earth I would have died. It snatched me from the Christian world as sure as loam and heat and sexual pleasure make the maize. I was pollinated (Journals).

Stylistically, Le Sueur's poetry reflects a successful use of symbols in a non-Western, Indian manner. Her symboling process does not reflect the western interpretation of symbols as standing *for* something, or as analogies for either ideas or feelings. Instead, her works reflect the Indian use of symbols, unique to that cultural world view. A symbol used in this way creates a process which evokes a sense of presence in the here and now and experience of participation in the energies which drive all being. Symbols do not merely mediate between the real and the ideal, but instead express that unity as it truly exists — in balance and harmony, in vital tension to create the *real*.

Symbol-making in this sense allows simple images to evoke a participation with the reality. We are caught up in the experience of the process itself, taken for a moment to T.S. Eliot's "still point of the turning world." We become all things, and participate in that understanding. Reading one of Meridel's poems, we experience the poem, as we do reality, from a variety of perspectives: now we *are* the earth speaking; now the reader listening; now the Indian people; now the mother, brother, sister. We are all these things, the poem is all these things and the symbols and imagery reflect the poet's experience of the oneness of all reality.

In the poem "Run Run Come Come," the "I" of the poet takes on a myriad of postures:

I am horizon that runs from your central breast
Curve you in embrace
Central where you left the skull and tree and the
    blood on sacrificial grass.
In my white buffalo robe
    I rise from all massacres.
I am the heat, I am your brave heart.
I am the scalp in your hand.
I am the severed arm speaking
    the amputated limbs
        the frozen mothers
The babes drinking at the frozen breasts.
I am rising from the bloody carnage
I am the ghost of Blunt Knife's Band going north
I am Black Hawk's song
I am a woman warm in the herbage of your embrace.
I was your child beside your thigh.
I am your sister beside you
    bone and sinew
        skin and skull
Running from the tide of gunshot.
Run run come come
For my sake let us arrive together.
Dig me from the cougared dust
Where I lie waiting you in fire and thorn.
From my feet burst the prairie grasses.
Do not withhold your strength or your power.
Our beauty comes from the generosity of your loins
Fed by antelope and deer   let your blood bloom
    at the sights of maidens.
Run run come come
The same enemy pursues us
    the same mother guards us
Run into my flowering prairie
      run   run.   (RAR, 5).

The earth here is the subterranean voice, exhorting, telling, identifying for the reader her connections with bone and sinew, skin and skull, songs and love, death, defeat, sorrow, but also endurance to struggle on, ultimately sparking our realization of the simultaneity of all experience.

In all Le Sueur's writings the images of the land as the great circle of the prairie interpenetrate with her imagery and words of politics, philosophy and sexuality. The emphasis on harmony and participation with the land require the appreciation of and participation with Woman, to complete the consciousness of the land in its fullest and deepest sense.

The earth is the woman raped; the raped woman is the earth. The exploited land is the worker exploited, the woman abused. She returns again and again to the process of merging these ingredients: earth, people, and women.

Understanding the earth as feminine requires that we look inside to the inner experience and feel ourselves as we are in that place — within the body, within the curve of prairie circle. The experience is of being within the circle, within the bowl, within the earth and all of nature. As we move into this earth consciousness, we experience the analogous sense of participation in our personal bodies, in our social structures and our personal relationships. The Christian rejection of the bodily, the material, the *mater*, left Western man outside of the process of nature, as alienated from it as he was from Woman. Part of our acceptance of and love for Indian literature is that it allows us to return to the body, to the land as feminine, restoring our sense of unity and harmony with nature.

This sense of participation and celebration of the material in a higher spiritual experience dominates Meridel's understanding of the earth and humanity's relationship with her. In "The Girl," Meridel documents the shift in perception which allows us to arrive at this "new" consciousness of oneness and relationship with the land.

The story begins with a woman traveling west alone, driving through the Tehachapi Mountains. "She had read up on the history of the mountains and listed all the Indian tribes and marked the route of the Friars from the Sacramento Valley . . ." She is tourist, she is looking *at* the land, seeing it objectively. "But before long she was sorry she had come through the Tehachapi Mountains. Why hadn't someone told her they were like that? They did her in. Frightening. Mile after mile in the intense September heat, through fierce mountains of sand, and bare gleaming rock faces jutting sheer from the road . . ." A change comes over her and the land begins to influence her experience, intruding on her tight reality. It comes slowly live, stepping off the front of the picture postcard she carries in her mind. "She drove very slowly, and something began to loosen in her, and her eyes seemed to dilate and darken as she looked into the fold upon fold of earth flesh lying clear to the horizon." As the story continues, the imagery of the earth grows richer, more feminine, more enfolding and encompassing. The land comes alive, and the woman moves into the land. "It began to affect her curiously. The earth seemed to turn on the bone rich and shining, the great mounds burning in the sun, the great golden body, hard and robust, and the sun striking hot and dazzling." The girl (who now has a passenger) is then seen in interaction with the earth, moving with it, joining in the experience with the land. "They rose on that vast naked curve into the blue blue sky, and dropped into the crevasse and rose again on the same curve. Lines and angles, and bare earth curves,tawny and rolling in the heat." "They fell down the valley, yellow as a dream. Then hills lifted themselves out of the edge of the night. The great animal flesh jointed mountains wrought a craving in her. There was not a tree, not a growth, just the bare swelling rondures of the mountains, the yellow hot swells, as if they were lifting and being driven through an ossified torrent." Finally, at the end of the story, the girl begins to understand her experience. "They didn't say anything about that in the books. She felt suddenly as if she had missed everything. She should say something more to her classes. Suppose she should say — 'the Tehachapi Mountains have warmed and bloomed for a thousand years.' After all, why not? This was the true information" (TG).

In Meridel's more mature poems, this sense of the earth as a living being and part of a process is even more pronounced. She speaks of the earth as something she can hold: "I am luminous with age. In my lap I hold the valley" (RAR, 25), as she speaks with the voice of an Indian woman. With another voice, she is the earth herself speaking, asking: "I have prepared a smoke for you husbands fathers brothers hunters. Restore thou for me my bruised body, Restore my bleeding feet to fruit" (RAR, 12). Or again, in an angry voice, warning: "Do not plow my flesh any more. Do not impregnate me without intention and love. I wander about Beware of me White Slavers I do not rattle before I strike" (RAR, 8).

But mostly, in these poems, we are left with a wonderful sense of the power of the feminine land in its most nurturing, caring, all encompassing sense. In the secure embrace of the great earth mother we experience the enduring, on-going optimism of the great cycles of season, the warm comforting rhythms of birth and growing things. Rejecting any and all perceptions of the land that would deny its reality and presence, Meridel has found a center from which to celebrate the earth as a sacred space. Her writing, and her life, resonate to the rhythms of the Middle Valley. A friend writes:

> Except for Mexico, she has never left her country. She moves through it by bus, even at 80, unwearied by the "hassle." She has an enormous physical energy and can lie down and sleep wherever she lies her head.
> What sustains this energy is love. An unbounded, almost indescribable love for the land, for the country, for its people, for its history, for its potential. Except perhaps Walt Whitman, nobody has sung the song of the land as passionately as Meridel. For nobody loved it, or sensed it, or felt it so profoundly. Prairies, rivers, oceans, fields of corn. You look at Meridel in her ripe age and have the strange feeling, "she is the land, she is the land in the time of its harvest." [6]

The Place of the People

> I came out of the secret pods of the midwest. Out of the village. It is the little place. We all emerge from the little place. We emerged from the Protestant village, from the white salt box houses. We emerged from these cellars also wounded. Yes, I felt the village (Film).

Meridel is a regional writer. Her commitment to her region — in particular the prairie spaces of the Midwest — is the quality which lends her work its rootedness and sense of ultimate connection and participation. A sense of place, according to many writers, is important to true artistic expression. Place can have many different meanings: it can merely describe the landscape at a superficial level; it can suggest a knowledge of not only the outer realities, but of the economy, the history, the religion and experiences of a people as they live on the land; it can imply a sense of psychic or psychological space. There are dangers, too, in a regional perspective: romanticizing the land and the people; a certain cuteness which reduces the heroic to the level of a travel brochure; and an indifference to the universal by emphasizing the local and the particular.

Meridel's regionalism avoids the pitfalls of a narrow perspective on place because she sees place not merely as geographic space, but that space as it is experienced by the people who live and create culture there. For her, roots are not just the physical place, but the people who love the land, or change the land, or even those who exploit the land. Roots need to be deep in the region — whether the region be a New York ghetto or the Kansas prairie. She writes:

> Corn cannot be international until it is in the kernel. It has to come from this land, this food, this farmer, this crop. Then you can scatter it all over the world as seed, as kernel. But it won't have any protein unless it is grown in native earth, soil in a particular spot (L).

The Midwest comes alive in Meridel's writings. We are drawn lovingly, at times with great sorrow, into the warm circle of the prairie. We are caught up in the harvest songs of the Midwestern people, in the exploding abundance of grain and corn. The rhythms of the seasons, of people and plenty, are rendered with great love and passion. The land and the people are one:

> All is made manifest in the harvest, an annunciation. All investing each other with reciprocal light and plenitude. It is all visible, the whole enacted in the valley. The common work in the man, woman, the village, community, the earth, the cosmos. All alive in the harvest. All is seen, all is known, all is plenty.
> This is an old and loved valley. It has not been bought and sold. Its love has been collective, its structure communal (Film).

Regionalism for Meridel meant not just the land, but the culture as it interrelated with the land. Often, the relationship was one of pain, or of fear:

> Like so many Americans, I will never recover from my sparse childhood in Kansas. The blackness, weight and terror of childhood in Mid-America strikes deep into the stem of life. Like desert flowers we learned to crouch near the earth, fearful that we would die before the rains, cunning, waiting the season of good growth. Those who survived without psychic mutilation have a life cunning, to keep the stem tight and spare, withholding the blossom, letting it sour rather than bloom and be blighted (CV, 7).

Meridel has always been sensitive to the interrelationships between the land and the people — the psychic impact of mutuality, in particular. Geographers are fond of teaching us about "mental maps" — our perceptual processes as they reflect our understanding of our land space. The mental map that Meridel has drawn for us of the prairie is a space that is in the "center" of a great continent, is one of a "global" consciousness, an expansive image which, from the center, perceives great land spaces all around. The *Christian Science Monitor*, in a review of *North Star Country*, commented: "The prairie and the ocean are now one. Another impossible has been accomplished. The circle is complete." [7]

The experience of the land does have a different feeling in the Midwest — a certain expansiveness, a spaciousness. Meridel has succeeded in translating that sense of wholeness and circularity and all-inclusiveness that marks the prairie tribes' relationship with the all-nurturing Earth Mother into a vision incorporating the land and the people. The prairie circle is the center place, the place, ultimately, from which the great life force itself keeps rhythms with the universe. Emerging from the little space on the prairie, the circle expands to the universal.

> Oh Kansas, I know all your little trees. I have watched them thaw and bud and the pools of winter frozen over, the silos and the corn-blue sky, the wagon-tracked road with the prints of hoofs, going where? And the little creeks gullying with delicate grasses and animals, the prairie dog, the rabbit, and your country with its sense of ruin and desolation like a strong raped virgin. And the mind scurrying like a rabbit trying to get into your meaning, making things up about you, trying to get you alive with significance and myth . . .
>
> Not going to Paris or Morrocco or Venice, instead staying with you, trying to be in love with you, bent upon understanding you, bringing you to life. For your life is my life and your death is mine also (CV, 24-25).

How Do We Love the Land: A Conversation

We had spent the day traveling up and down both sides of the St. Croix River in Minnesota and Wisconsin. Meridel called it her annual Spring trip. As we rode up and down ribbon roads, over the dark plowed land just beginning to green, we would stop here and there: the old cemetery in Prescott, the parks in Prescott and Hudson — all former "offices" where Meridel would take her typewriter and write. The offices were usually high over the river with a magnificent view in all directions. At each stop I would drag the dusty, worn out sleeping bag out of the car, and we would sit and visit for a while.

Neala: Well, Meridel, since the land is so important in your writing, I thought we could begin by talking about land and the American character. Perry Miller once said that there was something unique about the American experience with the land . . .

Meridel: They got some of it for the first time in history! Feudal people didn't own land. They loved the land, but it belonged to the landlord. The majority of people who came over here never owned land before in their lives.

N: Do you think they came to own it, in an individual way, or to share it? Private property and all that.

M: Not all of them. They didn't come to own it, they came to live on it. And they knew that there would be no feudal lord to put them off the land. I don't think it was just possession. It was to have food for their families, and not to have to bow to the landlord. Not to be thrown off the land (T4).

N: Well then how did land come to be so concentrated in a few hands today? How come more people didn't keep this free land?

M: All the wealth was based on the land, its resources. The government made land grants and the speculators coveted them into empires. Such grants totaled 75 million acres in lands of the Mississippi River valley and in so-called swamp lands. These "swamp land" grants, begun in 1849, were used by land speculators and railroad corporations that held that one-eighth of the lands of the Northwest Territory were swamp lands, and claimed them. Farmers buying back this land paid an estimated $50 million for land the speculators had picked up for less than $7 million. Railroad grants in Iowa alone equalled the size of two eastern states (WR, 44).

N: How did the speculators get the land? I mean, some people did get free land in the Homestead Act. How did they lose it?

M: Well for a homestead, you had to build a cabin within a year or something. But they didn't say what proportion. They'd build two-inch cabins and claim the land! They'd hire people to come out and claim the land. After the Civil War the railroads actually stole the land through congress, millions of acres just given to the railroads. They would just hire 50 people to sign up for the land and claim it that way. False deeds, false signatures. But what really stymied the democratic growth and development of the land was the mortgage. You got that 160 acres, but the vultures were sitting right there. Karl Marx pointed that out. He said that the land would be back in the hands of the bankers in five years. He was right, that was about what happened. Because when you went out there you had nothing. You had to have a plow, and they were sitting right there waiting, for 20 percent interest.

Powell, Lincoln's Secretary of the Interior, was asked to speak when they made North Dakota a state. He told them they should never plow the land on the plains. If you plow it up, it'll be blowing away. He said they should have a five year mortgage. If you never gave a mortgage except a 5-year mortgage, you wouldn't have the disasters on the plains. There is only three years of rain out of five on the plains, and the banks count on that. In the two years with no rain, they snatched up the land (T4).

Our lives have been rented at high interest. Our magnetic fields sold like daughters to high interest and international bankers. Leaching and pollution of the soil. . . .the loving abundance turned into greed (Journals).

N: Well, was there any collective actions on the land? Or

did the people go under one by one, losing their individual
plots of land?

M: Well of course there was collective activity on the
land! Those many utopian communities. They tell you
they weren't very important. But they were. Even the
first harvesters were collective. Nobody owned a har-
vester. They'd start in Oklahoma and go north. Even
today. The land grant colleges. They were set up to
develop the right strains and local varieties of the crops.
That was done communally, the colleges and the farmers.
When the Russians came over (in the 50's) they were
amazed. They hadn't arrived at anything quite like that
in the Soviet Union, that collective. That's the way that
the real creative mothering agriculture was developed in
America. Even the concept of the Homestead Act was not
just a concept of private ownership of the land. One-
hundred-sixty acres meant you had to learn to work it
collectively, even the collective use of machinery (T4).

N: But there weren't just all those collective things happen-
ing, either. You've written a lot about the greedy people, the
ones who came to exploit and destroy. You've really
documented that greedy eye in "Tradesman La Salle." The
idea of the empty land was not often just to feed families, it
was done in the spirit of adventure and greed that men
came, backed by European businessmen.

M: Yes. La Salle took with him chroniclers, priests,
notaries and clerks, but there is only truth in poets.
America was discovered by an eye that conquered the
gold, the silver, copper, the land, the oil; but what the poet
might have discovered has not been discovered. So it is
not known what was *felt* in that delicate country that was
just being "discovered," and was so hard to "get." Men
have gone grim because of this. Discovery is a subtle
experience. By the will alone it breeds a death whose seed
falls for many generations making the continent powerful and physical and brash, but keeping the soul from
rising, decomposing it into mechanical activities but

with the blood putrescent (TLS, 34). Mid-America was a tradesman's paradise. La Salle himself, the new industrial King, the first Rotarian (TLS, 35).

N: It seems that even in our pre-history the conquerers were tainted by this linear thinking. They only took the land, and never loved it.

M: Right. You look at this landscape and you see a predator just disappearing through the grass. You see a madman with a curious gunsight through a small hole of ownership. He has looked at this vast space. He has reduced it to his pocket (Journals).

N: Do you think that maybe part of our heritage is also this history — the greedy ones? It makes us a bit uneasy to accept these madmen and occupiers, I think. D.H. Lawrence once said that the "American landscape has never been at one with the white man. Never. And white men have probably never felt so bitter anywhere, as here in America, where the very landscape in its very beauty seems a bit devilish and grinning, opposed to us."⁸

M: If you remember, the story continues with the encounter between La Salle and his Indian guide: Nika laughed . . . "You are doing a murder, La Salle." "What? And not a man lost?"

Four generations will know that there has been a murder here, done in the beginning. They will feel it along their spines, the tentacles of murder in the dark empty air. They will know that something happened in the dark of America, in the womb (TLS, 55).

(Meridel sighed). Did you leave any message in the green land? Did you write anything in corn kernels? I never heard any of them speak of loving the land. Oh, you couldn't pull it out of them — like pulling teeth. How it happened, or any gleam, or love for it. Like many marriages, in contract only, in the dark. The landscape silent. Down your gunsights at last — not a red man, not a black man, not a bird, not a dove, not an antelope, not a

buffalo. Nothing moved. At last you had it empty. Only
the skull, your own, grinning into the ledger (Journals).
Yes, those greedy people were here. But many loved the
land. Not everyone was like that.

*N: I guess I don't have much faith that people love the land
anymore. Perhaps all the early settlers were like that —
getting and grabbing and conquering. Like the day we went
to Plainview to show the film, and some of the rural people
asked if the people in the city loved the land the way they do.
I said yes, but something in me wondered, doubted.*

M: The land is always there. Even in the city, the earth is
underneath. It'll come bubbling up!

N: Taking over the curbs?

M: She laughs. You'll find her sitting on the curb!

N: But did the people really love the land?

M: People were in ecstasy! People described coming out
of the forest when they came into Ohio. It must have been
an experience that put forward the spirituality of man.
It's in all the old literature. They experienced actual
wonder coming out of that forest.

It's like that old Spanish man I met who was on the
Poor People's march. He was sitting next to me on the
bus. He had never been out of his village in Northern
New Mexico. I think he felt something. And we came into
Missouri, and it was Spring. And he was sitting right
next to me, and the tears were just falling, just sitting
there without sobbing, like Indians cry. I watched them
fall for quite a while and finally I reached over and put
my hand on his knee and I said, what *is* it? And he said,
the green. How long does it go? Where does the desert
return? The green, he said. Think of the cattle. Think of
my sheep.

N: What a marvelous feeling he had for the land!

M: Well I still feel that a great power in the development
of America was the love of the land, and the terrific gift

that the land was to the immigrants. Capitalism had to conquer the land. But I think it's wrong to say the people did. Even the frontiersmen — Boone loved the land, Crockett loved the land. I think they all did. I don't think it's correct to interpret history that Imperialism was the only power there was. I think there was a tremendous impulse to develop the land communally and democratically. Those utopian communities. They weren't failures like they're made out to be. They were great spiritual communities. And it's still alive, the idea that they represented. They never failed.

And the Indian cultures here. Jimmy Durham, the Indian Marxist, is developing the idea that capitalism and private enterprise had a terrible time of it when they came here. He argues that there were many more Indians than we thought — perhaps up to 80 millions. And these communal cultures stood squarely in the way of the capitalists. They were so communal, they didn't know they could sell the land. They represented a great opposition to the free enterprise system and the development of capital. They had to physically destroy the communal idea of the Indian and the pioneer in order to move into the land. They never did defeat the Indians militarily. They spent more in the Indian Wars than they've ever spent on any war since, except the Second World War.

N: *Let's talk for a while about the "feminine" as it relates to the land. I can't really think of any American writers who look at the land in a feminine way. In fact, I can't think of too many who see the earth as female, as Earth Mother, in the way that you do.*

M: Well the whole philosophy of the last century in literary circles was male. I'm not worried any longer about being called "romantic." Or unrealistic. You don't have to argue any more, or document that the linear, practical, real, progressive world is death. It's obvious. You can't progress in energy mechanically without coming to disaster. That's what we've come to. And the idea that energy is endlessly multiplied and you can rape it forever certainly has been proven wrong. Those books (here she is referring to the books discussed in this chapter). They just talk about the land as object, they don't talk about the relationship. And of course, they don't believe in the democratic element, except Turner. They don't believe in the people at all, so there's no movement in their philosophy, there's no struggle between the development of capitalism and the development of democracy, so they don't see the land either as a relationship of struggle and change.

N: Do you think that with things like the "back to the land" movement, that things are changing, that maybe we're returning to a loving relationship with the land?

M: I didn't ever say go back to it, I said don't leave it! And you can't leave it. If you don't go back to the land, or back to corn, you're going to die. You're going to blow it up, it's that simple. Either value it or blow it up. I used to feel very apologetic about my beliefs, but I don't anymore.

N: It's really almost fashionable today, even with the radical writers about the land, to say that we're alienated from it.

M: You may hate it or deny it, but you still have to eat from it. It's like your mother's breast. You may hit her with your fist, but you still have to suck.

N: Well I'm still skeptical. Maybe we have lost some of our sense of relationship with the land. Maybe we need to be taught, or to re-teach each other about the love of the land.

M: (She gets angry.) The dream of America yet — of every factory worker and middle class person — what do they do when they get any money? They go out of the city and have a little piece of land. Those intellectual concepts are so — you can play games with ideas, and they're all true. But they're not the synthetic truth, or the whole truth. I often think that people who say those ideas — I just look at them and see that they're leaving their bodies out. If they ever consulted their stomachs, or their genitals, or their liver, they would have entirely different concepts. All the things they say, they don't seem to be connected with anything. Not even themselves!

N: Some of your critics have suggested that there's a "mystical" quality about your writing about the land.

M: I don't think it's mystical. That's the whole thing about the real and the practical. That's something you have to break down. The "real" and the "practical" is the mystical! Our feeling of what is reality is the relationship and the love of the land and the relationship with the land — and that's not mystical. Let's turn it around and say that the linear is the "mystical." It had absolutely no reality, no substance, no body. They've destroyed millions of bodies, they destroyed the water, the air, and the land, because *they're* unreal, bodily and "mystical." But the real and the practical leads to conception and birth, and food from the earth, and nourishment — not destruction. The destruction has become the fantasy and the neurotic. Let's make them say *they're* the unreal! (T4).

Rachel: I think what Meridel would say is that none of these destructive concepts could exist if the land belongs to all of us, for our use, while we live. And you can't do that with private ownership of the land. We confuse things sometimes. Like not having private ownership of the land doesn't mean that as an individual I won't want to have a place to be, or have space around me where I can walk and breathe and live. What is really "unreal" is that we can think "buying" that space, and then have a piece of paper that describes that space, and if I own it, it's all right. That's impossible! The only possibility is this give-and-take, that all of us get to walk and breathe. Russell Means argues — and I'm oversimplifying — that man is the only being on earth that doesn't know his role in relationship with the rest of nature, and that his task is to figure out his role, to be in balance with the rest of nature, which is already in balance (T9). [9]

N: I agree that it's not enough for people to just have a sense of their private plot of earth — that they have to have an understanding of the interrelationships of all nature. But I'm not so sure that people are hearing that, or doing that. They just keep on destroying. For most of us, it's not even a matter of doing something for ourselves, but like the farmers, we poison in order to stay alive in a competitive world. Or, to use another example, the poisons that we have created in order to make life easier — like xerox copies use terrible chemicals.

M: I think the people are beginning to know what's happening, and they're defending nature. I don't know why you say that. You haven't lived in a dark age where no one was speaking for the land. What you don't believe is that everybody is responding. You think only you're responding. You don't believe that there's an electrical charge — something like Tesla's ideas — that when one magnetic field vibrates, the whole earth vibrates. Everything is like that — reacting. That's a physical fact now, like what I said when I was young. And it isn't romanticism. That's a scientific fact — the vibratory sensitivity of everything. In the same way you can't ring a beautiful bell here and it doesn't resound everywhere. Everybody resounds. It doesn't depend on a bunch of intellectuals exposing something, or saying it. People have been resounding to this all along. That idea that you're the only person resounding. Nonsense. How pretentious can you get? Maybe you're just resounding from sombody else. They gave you the tone and you picked it up. Maybe you didn't originate it at all. The intellectual just puts a net over all of that and by his linear logic can prove out the world. And all the time he may be ringing himself (T4).

74

ENDNOTES

These ideas are manifest in a wide variety of modern experiences. The contemporary ecology movement and the consciousness of nature as a force outside of the control of man has generated a spate of "ecological disaster" movies, where nature strikes back; the current debate over genetic manipulation; the "creature from the black lagoon" who is evil inherent, and the like. Also, curiously, we might connect our rejection of "natural" processes in our culture to the subconscious rejection of nature as evil. We go to great pains, for example, to cover up our bodily odors with "herbal" essences — an irony of sorts. We could also give numerous examples of rejection of bodily pleasures and sexual gratification and repression of some of our more "natural" processes as signs of this inability to accept nature on her own terms.

William Burch, *Daydreams and Nightmares* (New York: Harper & Row, 19710, pp. 105-106.

Walt Whitman,*Leaves of Grass and Prose Works*, Ed. Mark Van Doren (New York: Viking, 1955), p. 692.

Meridel Le Sueur, Rachel Tilsen, and Neala Schleuning, Conversation taped September 1976. Rachel (Meridel's daughter).

Octavio Paz, in *Seven Voices* (New York: A. Knopf, 1973), p. 243.

Irene Paull, Letter received May 10, 1976.

Christian Science Monitor, Book Review, January, 1946.

D.H. Lawrence, quoted in Thomas E. Sanders, *The Writer's Sense of Place: A Symposium and Commentaries*. *South Dakota Review*, 13, 3 (Autumn, 1975), p. 109.

Also Russel Means, "Native American Spiritual Values," April 4, 1974, 1974 Radio Address. Minnesota Public Radio, Audio Archives No. A116.

"Let Us Seek Each Other In the Villages of the Earth"

For over two hundred years, American history has been dedicated to examining varying shades of our white, Protestant, capitalistic culture. All other histories — minority history, radical history, labor history, women's history — were inconsequential — a lengthy footnote at best. But people are now examining those footnotes, those half-obliterated footprints of our radical heritages, and a certain common, yet persistent thread is emerging from American history — the vital history of the people and their work, their struggle to survive.

> The heritage they give us is the belief we have in them. It is the story of their survival, the sum of adjustments, the struggle, the folk accumulation called sense and the faith we have in that collective experience. It was real and fast, and we enclose it. Many unknown people lived and were destroyed by it. What looks to us grotesque or sentimental is the humor of the embryo, the bizarreness of the unformed, and the understanding of it as a prerequisite to our survival. It was real, and created our day. Perhaps it encloses us. It is the deep from which we emerge.
>
> Like a lion the people leave marks of their passing, reveal that moment of strength when the radicle plunged into the soil, in a fierce struggle on a strong day, and a nation held (NSC,11).

Part of the difficulty in illuminating the radical roots of American democracy lies in the perpetuation of certain myths about radical politics — myths which were, more often than not, deliberately distorted and perverted to incite and inflame the endemic paranoia in the dominant culture. The fear of the "other" and of the "unknown" expressed in political terms has come to mean "radical." Radical thought in our history has always had a touch of the "devil" associated with it. It was evil, and a threat to the community, the family and the very moral foundations of WASP society. The fear of the unknown was nourished by myths that radical thought was "foreign," or "old world" — polluted with un-American ideologies. The new world must remain unpolluted and pure beyond ideology.

Being a radical in America has always been an exercise in courage. At times secretly admired, at others publicly hounded and harassed, the role of a radical has been a difficult one.

> . . . in its nervous conservatism, America too often dismisses its revolutionaries as bizarre by definition, forgetting that a revolutionary, utopian streak runs through the fabric of American history like a color through a plaid, sometimes dim, sometimes bold, but always a part of the design.[1]

Emma Goldman, a turn-of-the-century radical feminist and anarchist, would echo similar thoughts as she reflected on her own experience as a radical.

> It struck me that behind the difference between American and French legal procedure was a fundamental difference in attitude to social revolt. Frenchmen had gained from their revolution the understanding that institutions are neither sacred nor unalterable, and that social

conditions are subject to change. Rebels are therefore considered in France the precursors of coming upheavals.

In America the ideals of the Revolution are dead — mummies that must not be touched. Hence the hatred and condemnation which meet the social and political rebel in the United States.[2]

The solution to the problem of radicals of Goldman's era was to deport hundreds of them back to their native countries. A wave of the hand and poof! WASP purity was preserved and the evil had been exorcised.

It was this wave of radical activity at the turn-of-the-century that highlighted America's love-hate relationship with revolutionary politics. This time, WASP fears were well grounded. Myth coincided with reality. There really were foreigners, hundreds of thousands of them, and they really did bring all those radical ideologies to the pure American Eden. They came — many of them escaping conscription, many indoctrinated with the "new" ideas of Karl Marx, many with firsthand fighting experience in the political struggles which shook Europe from 1848 onward. They came with "revolutionary" and "radical" hopes of realizing their own ideals of freedom and happiness. But they discovered, upon their arrival, that while the "new" thought had preceded them, it was by no means universal or accepted by WASP Americans. There was no room in the American inn, and the newcomers were crowded into ghettos in the large industrial cities, and were exploited beyond their wildest dreams by a burgeoning capitalist revolution.

These "huddled masses" quickly learned to organize, however, and in the process, established a new identity — one which challenged the WASP view of how "Americans" ought to act. They organized. They picketed and they marched. And they fought for what they felt were "real" American, democratic goals: decent wages, an eight-hour working day, the right to organize into unions, the right to speak out politically and collectively. Their confrontation with American values was a violent one. They fought and died for their beliefs at Ludlow, in Chicago's Haymarket Square, in the teeming cities of the East Coast. Their era nourished literally hundreds of groups, sects, movements, collectives — Eugene Debs, Bill Haywood and Elizabeth Gurley Flynn and the Wobblies, the Anarchists, Socialists, Populists — all commited to changing the political reality of American culture. The new revolution was launched, attacking all totems of the WASP culture.

WASP America was galvanized into action. The dominant culture set to work Americanizing the new foreigners — giving them baths, cutting their hair, insisting they speak English, give up their "foreign" ideologies and cultures, and melt into the melting pot of American individualism. After all, the Red Man and the Black Man has been assimilated or beaten into submission, and the integration of the new, more white Americans was seen as a similar challenge.

Historians of this era have sought to minimize the importance of these radical movements, choosing to gloss over or ignore the contributions of militant groups like the farmer's Grange, the women at Seneca Falls or the Wobblies. Instead, they focused their attention on the Progressives — liberal intellectuals whose goal was to "reform" America and fight the war to save Democracy. In recent years, however, we are coming to understand our radicals and rebels in new terms. It seems somehow ridiculous, for example, to suggest that all the Blacks, all the Indians and women, or all those collectives and communes of white, middle-class American young people either love America or "leave it." Criticism of WASP culture is coming from many directions, and today our rebel speaks not just for him or herself, but for communities of people, cultures, economic affinity groups and other critics of the status quo — all of whom have visions of a new and different American democracy.

The ideological inspiration for this recent radical political activity has been primarily Marxist in orientation. Whether in terms of Communism, Anarchism, Socialism, or collective political ideology, there are common threads running back to the Communist Manifesto. These ideologies all subscribe to a few basic tenets: to be radical is to proclaim a pluralistic instead of a centralist interpretation of the contours of American culture; a commitment to looking beyond the patristic, nuclear family to the communal family; a rejection of concepts of private property and consumerism; adoption of a more ecological, participatory attitude to both things and nature; the rejection of a hierarchical social order and acceptance of a more collective, participatory political process, and an emphasis on developing connection and love as the basis of human communication.

Radical democracy also challenged the individualistic bent of traditional democracy. In its recognition of classes and collectives, it redefined the idea of "rights." In traditional democracy, rights were extended to individuals only — only as a unit of one were you recognized by the state. The various versions of American radicalism offered an alternative to individualism: "it introduced a new principle of human fellowship based upon the common body of cooperative labor, a principle corresponding not to private ownership but to the social character of production.[3]

American radicalism was not confined to a narrow economic analysis, however. The meaning of radical took on broader, deeper connotations. In the tradition of American Transcendentalism, American rebels had always had a deep reverence for a holistic way of thinking — an organic sense of reality that challenged the linear, progressive rationalist world view. No longer could political questions be analyzed separately from all of reality. For the first time, we were challenged to confront the real implications of a world of connectedness and interrelationship. No longer could Americans deny the web that held together politics, religion, racism, sexism. In the circle of political reality, the connections existed, good or bad, and demanded a response.

It is this connotation of radical that affords new insights into the history of the American people, and in particular, the role of Meridel Le Sueur. Although she never called herself an anarchist, her affections and affinities with those proud, creative revolutionaries bear amazing resemblances. Like Emma Goldman, Meridel has endured the wrath and hostility of the WASP culture, and to some extent, other radical groups. She has struggled to expand her understanding of our radical heritage through her writings and her activities over the past half century. Never content to rest with a particular ideology, she has opened up new vistas of thought and in the process, illuminated something very uniquely American.

Meridel's Political Philosophy

Le Sueur's political philosophy is a uniqe contribution to American anarchist theory. Most 20th century anarchist theory can be traced to two 19th century European intellectual traditions: libertarians trace their roots to the liberal tradition with its emphasis on *laissez faire* capitalism and individualism, while communist anarchists draw upon Marx's economic theories and class analysis. Seldom have American anarchists explored new, strictly American sources of this intellectual and activist tradition. Le Sueur's midwestern feminist anarchism merits attention for its unique integration of feminism, American Indian philosophies, and Marxism.

Le Sueur is perhaps best known as a writer — and most especially as a "political" writer. It is only in recent years that attention has been drawn to the philosophical context from which her writing emerged. Her lifelong political involvement has, of course, generated much analysis and debate — particularly her activities during the 30s. Her involvement with the Literary Left[4] has been variously mourned by those who saw a good writer go "down the Communist drain" and celebrated by those who would claim her for a particular ideological stance. A closer examination of her life and her unpublished writings, however, suggests that her political roots can be traced to the development of anarchist ideas in a midwestern context. Drawing on both her personal and her political/cultural heritage, Le Sueur has woven together in her philosophy those dropped strands of a particularly midwestern variety of anarchism.

The Midwest

These men have emerged from the old roots of American democracy, from the injurious silence and struggle, from world Marxism. You have

never seen exactly such men before. You have never seen me before. I
have been borned and saved by these struggles and the sight of each
other. Discover comrades and discover yourself (Journals).

It is difficult to find words to describe the midwestern
radical experience. Radical histories tend to focus on the
European foundations of American radicalism or the eastern
urban experience, or the activities of specific working class
organizations, such as the IWW. The midwest (and the south
and west for that matter) are dismissed as "populist" areas,
where populism is portrayed as a middle class movement.
Richard Hofstaedter in the *Age of Reform*, forever, it would
seem, has condemned the midwest to radical oblivion. A closer
examination of the midwest experience, however, suggests
that a unique radicalism appeared early in the culture.

Radical European politics did not, as we assume, begin
with the publication of Marx's Communist Manifesto in 1848.
In the early 19th century political unrest was widespread in
Europe, and a host of competing ideologies sought to articulate the new revolutionary consciousness. (Many early anarchists, as we know, often did not even refer to themselves
consciously with that title — choosing rather to merely
differentiate their ideologies from other's in the ongoing
debates.) Sorting out the roots of ideological strains becomes a
giant puzzle for the historian of ideas.

Traditional political analysts generally find a "line" of
thinkers to which we dutifully trace the ideas under examination. To understand Meridel, however, we need to look not
only at ideas which might have influenced her — Marx is an
obvious mentor, Christopher Caudwell another — but also to
the radical cultures of the midwest which, by her own
reflection, inspired her thinking and her political activism.
Her political ideas are a distillation rather than direct, linear
descendents, and as such they represent a growing and
changing political culture.

I believe early in my life I saw two things: one, the dangers and cruelty
of the predator. This was learned as well and instinctively as the deer
learns about the man with the gun. Secondly, I saw the land and the
people squeezed in this vice of capitalistic production which was
counter to their own deep democratic needs and knowledge. I saw the

land polluted and the people destroyed. I allied myself to the struggles of the oppressed. (L).

The midwest was a likely setting for the development of anarchist ideas.[5] In the East, anarchist thought was dominated by libertarian anarchists such as Benjamin Tucker, Josiah Warren and others building on traditional liberal impulses of individualism and anti-monopolism.[6] In the urban ghettoes was found a more "European" anarchism, primarily economic — an ideology committed to the working class movements and syndicalist economics — growing out of an active struggle against exploitation and starvation in the cities of the new land. The unsettled prairies and plains of the midwest, however, represented a different economic environment in which developed a culture based on decentralization, collectivism, anti-authoritarism and anti-clericalism. The vast physical distances between pioneer communities encouraged decentralization. Economic exploitation and land speculation by Easterners served to nourish as well, the strong anti-authoritarian tendencies associated with the anarchist thought. Settled largely by Europeans, the midwest was also generally ignorant of the individualist philosophical anarchists of the Eastern American tradition. Equally distant were the economic problems of an industrial society and the political need for mass organizing of the large urban populations. What emerged instead on the prairies and plains was an integration of pre-Marxist Socialism and the experiences in agrarian community, creating prairie anarchism.

By far the largest European group to emigrate to the midwest were the Germans — many of whom were disenchanted radicals escaping the 1848 revolution and conscription to European armies. These "Forty-Eighters," [7] educated and articulate professional people, built towns, established utopian collectives, and published newspapers promoting their pre-Marxian socialist ideas. Many formed Turnverein, or Turner Societies, where they settled. The Turners promoted a strong anti-clerical, anti-lawyer, free-thinking philosophy which has influenced midwestern culture to this day. The commitment to grass-roots pluralism and suspicion of centralized authority kept many German communities isolated until after World War One. These Germans also tended to take "un-American" stands supporting such issues as women's rights, abolition, and pacifism. Long-standing WASP hostility to the independent and free thinking German communities surfaced to fuel repression of the IWW and other radical groups during and after World War I, when it was charged that radicals were German inspired and controlled.

In the writings of the St. Louis Movement philosophers[8] such as William T. Harris, W.D. Howiston, Henry Brokmeyer, Susan Blow and others can be found a formalized expression of the Turner ideas as well as the more radical ideas of Forty-Eighters such as Wilhelm Weitling and Karl Heinzen. These American Hegelians were especially influential in American education — the Kindergarten movement, free universities outside the academy, and the restructuring of higher education along the German seminar model.

Other immigrant groups brought similar ideas and practices to the midwest. The Hauge Movement, which had its roots in Norway's Peasant Party, later evolved into Christian Socialism in the midwest, and Youngdale notes that the Non-Partisan League was strongest in areas dominated by Norwegians. The Finns who settled the northern Minnesota forests were especially active in developing cooperatives. Along with the Slavs and the Italians they were later the base of IWW activities on the Mesabi Range in the iron mines.

In the early 20th century, the IWW in the midwest was strongly committed to an anarchist perspective.[9] The Wobblies, perhaps more than any other group, put into practice this prairie anarchism, and were an early influence in Le Sueur's ideological development. Anarchists, communists, dispossessed immigrant workers and unskilled agricultural laborers joined the One Big Union to secure workers' rights. The Wobblies refused to join any political coalitions, developing instead their own brand of syndicalism.

Although Chicago was a strong urban center for IWW activities, the agricultural workers and miners further west provided the numerical base for their strength. In the miners' struggles on the Mesabi Range[10], the organization of threshing crews across the plains, and the early anti-war, anti-draft movement[11], we see the traces of their impact.

A mythology has grown up in American culture about the Wobblies as the "singing" revolutionaries. Anarchism has, of course, always had an aesthetic/political integration as a hallmark of its philosophy, and Le Sueur is no exception as she recalls:

> I was nourished by this place and time and people. Through our house on Dayton Avenue in St. Paul there came the dissidents, the brave exploded root, the radicle. I think the IWW's had the greatest influence on me. They believed that only from the working class could come the poets and singers, the prophets, the heroes, and the martyrs (APNC, 43).

This image of joyous, singing radicals, however, also served to reinforce WASP perceptions of radicals as loose, immoral, and irresponsible. In the WASP mind, free thinking and free-love went hand in hand. German anti-clericalism took an interesting turn in midwestern anarchism as it was transformed into the anti-Puritanism response to WASP rigidity and lack of humor. The easterner, or "Yankee," was not only big monopoly and centralized power, but an "uptight" Puritan as well. The Germans, for example, found themselves in opposition to prohibition — and in the Anti-Saloon League propaganda of the early 20th Century, we find the saloon keeper is generally German or Scotch. The "Puritan" lacked the collective feel for Gemütlichkeit that characterized the immigrant communities, and the WASP community frowned on the free-thinking, non-church-going immigrants who partied and picknicked on Sundays. Much "Blue Law" legislation was anti-immigrant and anti-radical in intent, for example.[12]

Anarchist ideas have often been confused with prairie Populism. Populism has variously been interpreted as a "rural" movement, as a "petty-bourgeois" movement, and more recently, as a psychologically "ambiguous" movement.[13] Each of these interpreters has placed *every* midwestern, grass roots radical group under the Populist umbrella — resulting in even more ambiguity. Creative analysis of the roots of

Populist thought will separate out those ideas which are clearly anarchistic.

Those groups which can be identified as having an anarchist tendency, are, first of all, culture organizations which had a critique of capitalism at their ideological base. The IWW, the early Turners,[14] Wilhelm Weitling's followers, the Finnish cooperative movement, to name a few, were all built on collective, communal structures. Secondly, anarchist groups are characterized by a commitment to decentralization and local control — those groups which were clearly anti-state in their ideology. Many early cooperative movement groups were committed to creating a new social order, whereas groups like the Grange were committed to cooperative buying clubs without the social reorganization implicit in the co-ops. Midwestern anarchism walked the narrow plank of ideology that was essentially pre-Marxist, European based, but which underwent a subtle transformation in the small towns of the middle west.

It is this set of ideas which lies at the heart of Le Sueur's anarchism. Although historians have underestimated the force of these ideas, the uneasy blend of idealism and practicality are central tensions in midwestern American philosophy and contribute to a unique decentralized participatory political ideology. Le Sueur knew this history well, and as she herself moved through midwestern radical culture all her life, these ideas were integrated with her feminism, a later variety of Marxism, and American Indian philosophies, developing what she called the "circular" political consciousness.

The Politics of the Circle

Le Sueur's feminism has been explored in a previous chapter so I will concentrate here on the political dimensions of those ideas. By the time she was 20, the women's movement had packed up its bags and gone home after securing the vote. Over the years, Le Sueur developed her ideas independently of any widespread women's movement, and in the tradition of women like Emma Goldman she carried her ideas far beyond the "single-issue" politics of turn of the century feminists.

One important element of her political feminism was her life-long articulation of the women's reality. Very early in her writing career, she committed herself to expressing the culture of women. Her stories are rich in feminine metaphors and the female characters speak their concerns and experiences as women: birth, alienation from men and support of other women, care for their families, the joys and sorrows with other women.[15] Her identity as a woman was not only a personal one: women's experiences united them in a community which had obvious political implications.

Central to Meridel's feminism and political philosophy is her idea of the circle. The concept of circularity and cyclical return is an old one in Western thought. For Meridel, the circle takes on new meaning, however. The key to understanding the political implications of Le Sueur's circular consciousness, is the dialectical nature of the circle. The circle is not a rigid "cycle" in the classical sense, but dynamic, like a spiral, as in modern scientific theories of relativity. I call this new circular sense "dialectical relativity." There is much confusion over what dialectic means: it has generally been interpreted as the clashing of opposites. Dialectics, however, in its true modern sense implies a *relationship of interdependence*. There is, for example, in dialectical thinking, no subject, no object which is separate from or outside of the reality. Each is part of the other. You can't understand or isolate, or analyze anything separately. The implications for Le Sueur's politics, of course, are obvious: political theory cannot analyze the self *separate* from the collective, or outside of the circle. In this philosophy, the circle, and the collective, is the reality: it is not constructed or made, it simply is the way things are.

One of the most important political projections of her circular consciousness is a feminine concept of space; space enclosed and contained, yet space which bursts forth with creative energy. As many feminists know, Eric Erickson has polluted this sense of "inner space" by presenting it as narrow and limiting. But for Le Sueur, inner space is the circle understood on a personal level. The potential of the seed pod, the womb, the bowl or the earth itself are symbols she uses to depict space as "inner" — that space in which one centers the universe as a whole, and that space out of which one creates a reality which is infinitely expansive, containing all, birthing all.

Women have, I think, the wisdom of the earth. Everything is involved. That's why the Indians call it the Mother Earth. They don't mean it in the sense of mother the way we do, that is, giving birth — they mean the profound and absolute womb where everything exists and returns cyclically (T13).

The origins of American Indian influences in Le Sueur's thought are equally subtle. One of her grandmothers was an Iroquois, and we can speculate that her own heritage was one impetus to her integration of Indian philosophies into her own world view. The Iroquois have of course, contributed much to American democratic theory, and the strong political role of women in that culture served to reinforce Le Sueur's feminist views.

At a deeper level, Le Sueur's philosophy illuminates the subtle inter-connections between feminist ideas and the American Indian philosophies of the nature and the land. She has often acknowledged her intellectual/spiritual debt to the Sioux, the Hopi. the Iroquois and the Navaho, in particular. Her Indian-inspired metaphysic defines reality as the relationship with all that exists in both the material and the ideal world. Reality is not the Transcendental Oversoul (although there are affinities), nor pantheism, but that which emerges in the process of *relationship*.[16] John Fire illuminates the idea of interrelatedness and circularity as it is manifested in the Sioux culture:

To our way of thinking the Indians' symbol is the circle, the hoop... The camp in which every tipi has its place was also a ring. The tipi was a ring in which people sat in a circle and all the families in the village were in turn circles within a larger circle, part of the larger hoop which was the seven campfires of the Sioux, representing one nation. The nation was only part of the universe, in itself circular ... circles within circles, with no beginning and no end. To us this is beautiful and fitting, symbol and reality at the same time, expressing the harmony of life and nature. Our circle is timeless, flowing; it is new life emerging from death — life winning out over death.[17]

In the phrase "symbol and reality at the same time," lies a key to understanding the essence of Le Sueur's circular reality. In Western thought, symbols stand *for* something, as analogies for either ideas or feelings. In the Indian, and circular, consciousness, symbols are expressed differently:

> The words articulate reality — not "psychological" or imagined reality, not emotive reality captured metaphorically in an attempt to fuse thought and feeling, but that reality where thought and feeling are one, where objective and subjective are one, where speaker and listener are one, where sound and sense are one.[18]

For Meridel, it creates a special awareness and consciousness of the land, for example:

> The land becomes Indian. He sees it differently. He is not trying to own it, or cultivate it, receive from it something, steal from woman and land. He sees it burning. It moves into him, he moves into it... love enters you from the movement, from the speed, from the long celebration of the true mother, the earth. (Journals).

This dynamic sense of the circle and of reality is what binds Meridel's universe together in intimate relationship. Circularity means that we are all *in* and *of* the circle — nothing is external to reality. The reality *is* relationship. Things are known only in their relationship — their web of connection with all being. One cannot choose to be related; one *is* related — to all life, to the land, to people, to the universe. Relationship, therefore, is no longer a mere "coming together" but a necessity of our very being. There is no Self, separated and discrete. The individual is known only relative to others, and in fact, defines the self as it is in relationships. This sense of participation is similar to the Transcendentalists' concept of reciprocity, but in Le Sueur's thought, the individual is not lost in the Oversoul but is defined and becomes unique through the process of interaction. Such a metaphysic underlies the theory and practice of collectivist anarchism and requires a new orientation to such traditional concepts in western thought as personal property, the self, and political ideology.

Relationship As Property

At the root of anarchist thought lies a rejection of traditional concepts of property. Anarchism denounces private property (Capitalism), collective ownership of property (Marxism), consumerism (property for its own sake), and articulates, in general, a distrust of wealth and accumulated property of any sort. When property is discussed, it is in terms of creative use only, in terms of use-value rather than exchange or surplus value.

Proudhon's famous quotation, "Property is theft," forms the basis of one anarchist critique of property. More radical anarchists, however, criticize the idea of property itself — arguing that property is linked inextricably with the concept of domination and power. Max Stirner wrote: "Nevertheless, property is the expression for unlimited dominion over somewhat (thing, beast, man) which 'I can judge and dispose of as seems good to me.' "[19] In critiquing Marx, Stirner argued that it mattered little whether property was in the name of a State, Humanity, or any group or "society." The very act of making something "property" — the establishment of the value of a thing for something else — only served to perpetuate the process of exploitation and domination which are inherent in "property."[20] To Proudhon, Stirner retorted: "Is the concept 'theft' at all possible unless one allows validity to the concept of 'property'? How can one steal if property is not already extant?"[21] And he answered his own question: "If men reach the point of losing respect for property, every one will have property, as all slaves become free men as soon as they no longer respect the master as master."[22] According to Stirner, the only value to which we can make claim is what we can hold in our hands, i.e., what can be personally transformed by our creative work. Only those individuals with a highly developed sense of self-worth, self-valuing (his sense of "egoism") will be able to give up the idea of property as ownership.

Le Sueur's anarchist/feminism incorporates this same radical critique of property. As women, she believes, we understand not only the commoditization of the worker in the Marxist sense, but the deeper implications of property and ownership in terms of all relationships analyzed in terms of their power relations. We have been treated as "property" and we need to seek alternatives to that mode of relationship.

> The oppressor is a conquistador; he's an aggressor, a Caesar. He owns property. Everything to him is objects and property. Personally I don't think you can have a sexual relationship with a property owner. I don't think that's possible. I mean, you're just like the land, the earth, that he's going to sow and reap and make money out of. The woman is a property. There's no possible sexual relationship between a property owner and what he owns. That's why they call it the "missionary" position! The property is underneath and the property owner is on top. It's a relationship of the oppressor and the oppressed. It's a terrible relationship. Property relationship is the lowest, most terrible relationship there is in the world. Because it's seizure in the first place. How do you get it, how do you steal it? You've seized it. That's the only way that property is gotten (T13).

Therefore, to understand a relationship to property is to understand a power relationship — a relationship which is inherently unequal, hierarchical and hence exploitive.

> I think the main thing is the conquering. And it's related to rape and conquering women, and colonial conquering, genocide. It seems to me that in my philosophy, that's the key. It's the same — in relation to the land, to women, to the subjugation of everything (T4).

> What does an American think about the land, what dreams come from the sight of it, what painful dreaming? Are they only money dreams, power dreams? Is that why the land lies desolate like a loved woman who has been forgotten? Has she been misused through dreams of power and conquest? (CV,12).

Le Sueur struggled with this appropriative attitude even as it related to her writing and her use of language:

> Almost all my language comes from the English poets, the nature poets, all those bastards. When they look at a sunset, they look at nature like they do a woman — they want her, to possess her. Now I don't look at a landscape that way. (T5) How do I look at a landscape, how do you? I don't want to seize it. It's not a sexual thing — it's sexual, but not as a male conquistador looking to grab it, to have it. (Journals).

What Le Sueur demands is a new attitude toward reality that negates the idea of property itself. Things, objects, people, the land will no longer be understood in terms of their value as property, or have their reality defined in terms of property relationships. Instead, Le Sueur proposes we develop an intimate sense of relationship in a dialectical sense — a mutual regard for one another that respects the relationship itself as the essence of value. Things and people and land would only exist and have value as part of a process or praxis — in their interaction with one another.

There is no relationship possible if you are outside of one another. The relationship is like a lodge — all within the cult. You cannot touch a man or woman that is done up, insulated. There is no spark (Journals).

Relationship As Self

In addition to ideas of property, there is another powerful force in American culture which mitigates against this new sense of relationship — the value matrix which Le Sueur calls "Puritanism."

Puritanism was a trashing of the body, discipline of the body against anything that was pleasurable. Sin was very much a part of Puritanism — the witch trials were Puritan trials against women with sensuality. It was a whole religious and philosophical orientation away from the body, away from the earth.

We all feel that, whether we're Puritans or not. The trashing of the body and the senses. And especially your sexuality (T13).

Early in the development of her philosophy, Le Sueur saw the connections between her experiences as a woman and her political beliefs. The Anti-clericalism *cum* anti-Puritanism of the early prairie anarchists, reinforced with Le Sueur's feminist insights, formed a strong critique of the Puritan repression of the body.

The brutality to the body, to the feelings, the senses. . . this is a part of Puritanism which is necessary to capitalism. This is also related to criticisms of a lyrical, sensual kind of writing (which went against even the radical perceptions of my time. They felt there was something "seductive" in my writing — non-revolutionary, they thought!)

This has been one of the major restrictions of the oppressor class. They could not have had capitalism without this severe oppression of the body, of joy. Now more than ever they are afraid of this. They have to repress it. The living, loving person is a danger on the assembly line.[23] "You romanticize lust," they said about my writing. "Lust is horrible — only men have it." Beasts, lovely beasts with lust. But no. The Puritans hold it away in horror and then indulge in awful, unclean Romanticism. Talk about sex! A hen starving to death on a bushel of grain! (Journals).

Historically, some anarchists have expressed anti-Puritanism in a variety of ways: a celebration of spontaneity and excess, "Free Love" and "anti-work" philosophies, and a rejection of organizational structures which restrict free movement of mind and body. According to Le Sueur, repression of the body — evolving out Augustinean Christianity and transported to America via Puritanism — is an internalizing process of repression and exploitation. In a vivid passage from "Corn Village" Le Sueur describes this self-repression:

> She was embarrassed by any excess of feeling and had a way of turning down her lips bitterly. She had that acrid, bitter thing too about her body, a kind of sourness as if she had abandoned it. It was like an abandoned thing, perhaps it had not been occupied. The Puritans used the body like the land as a commodity, and the land and the body resent it. She never took a bath except under her shift. Hearing her move about her room alone I always wondered what she was doing, so bodyless, with that acrid odor as if she had buried her body, murdered it and buried it, and it gave off this secret odor revealing the place where it lay (CV, 20-21).

Emma Goldman called this process of self-repression her "internal tyrants."[24] In its deepest sense, "the personal is the political" extends even to the psychology of the individual woman and her internal dialogue. Self-inflicted oppression in its most insidious forms, Le Sueur believes, only aids external forms of oppression, reinforcing an imbalance of power.

Relationship as Politics

> As for the individual and the group: Joining has always been obnoxious to the bourgeois artist because of his false orientation to the middle-class groups and because such groups in an exploiting world are spurious and false groups, an accretion of individuals. An organic group pertaining to growth of a new nucleus of society is a different thing. You do not join such a group, you simply *belong*. You belong to that growth or you do not belong to it . . . You cannot "join" it in the ordinary middle-class sense as you can join the Rotarians or Kiwanis or any similar group. There are no organic groups in middle-class society because all groups are a subtle hypocrisy since capitalism is based on the exploiting ability of every individual against every other one (FO, 22).

Anarchism as a "political" ideology rejects traditional definitions of what is political. It is, in many ways, anti-political — and if there is one consistent pattern in anarchism it is the hostility to organization and structure based on centralization and hierarchy. Whether it be dogmatic thoughts, political institutions, or bureaucratic structures, at its core, anarchism rejects any relationship which is based on an inequality of power.

As an anarchist, Le Sueur is committed to decentralized collective activity as the primary political structure.[25] She believes that the sense of relationship is best developed in decentralized units which nourish the sense of intimacy between people and which are committed to collective, consensus decision-making. Instead of the large abstract concept of society, Le Sueur proposes more intimate social structures: the family, the neighborhood, the tribe, the village. These small structures nourish intimacy as a primary social value. The collective is, for Le Sueur, the basic political unit, and the dialogue which concludes this article develops her ideas of the collective process more fully.

The intimacy of a circular, collective organization of people calls for a different decision-making process. In Meridel's communal circle, there is no "right" process, no formula or prescription which will ensure that each and every decision will come about in the same way. Instead, collective decision-making rests on the faith that in the process of struggle, a consensus, a truth, acceptable to all, will emerge. To reason together in collectives is to find truth and actualize it in our individual, social and global communities.

> Life that has survived has never been the armoured and the aggressive. The duck, the butterfly and the bee have survived millions of years because they made communities, and formed cultural cohesions of mutual aid. . . The people alone can invoke the organization of knowledge for the good of mankind (WRF, 47).

The ethical implications of collective decision-making lie, of course, in the intimate relationship between means and ends. When the "personal is the political" the individual sense of intimate responsibility carries over to the responsibility for all. Consensus decision-making mitigates against an imbalance of power, it is assumed, since the goal is the good of all. For Le Sueur, truth has as many varied forms as the individual members of a collective. Meridel's long time friend,

Irene Paull, describes Meridel's individual processes of thought and action. These habits of mind in many ways parallel a collective decision-making process, and answer the question of how the reality of diversity and uniqueness can ever come to a political integration.

Perhaps what is most interesting and most frustrating about her is the kaleidescopic quality of her perceptions. She sees reality from so many different levels of perception that just when you think you agree with her or she with you, the kaleidescope turns to show an opposite shape or color. She sees the opposite of what she saw a moment ago. It is too much for an ordinary mind to follow. Something should be nailed down as truth, it's too uncomfortable in a world with nothing nailed down, with everything circular and rotating.

But Meridel quietly turns the truth around and looks at it from a totally conflicting side of it. . . The truth has a thousand sides and they keep appearing to her, first one side, then another. How can one pin down the truth when it is so kaleidescopic? And when there is no certitude?

Except one. More a conviction than a certitude. More an ideal to struggle for, to give one's life for, the belief that all men are created equal and endowed with equal rights to life, liberty and the pursuit of happiness. For this ideal she always felt it was worth fighting, struggling, submitting her individual need to the collective need, and she never stopped believing that some time, some way, we would as a species achieve this equality, learning to work collectively in order to survive as she believes animals work collectively to survive.[26]

Democratic goals, then, serve as one standard in Le Sueur's political formulations. She also posits as good, that people be equal, and that they work collectively to achieve the good of all. Another certitude in Le Sueur's circular world is her belief that growth which expands individual potential is "good." What threatens this growth and blights the process is "evil." An imbalance of power, however, seems to be the primary evil. Those forces and rhythms which maintain and perpetuate balance, however, are not found in institutions or laws or structures, but in the people themselves, as individuals functioning in collective process.

A Discussion about Collectives[27]

Neala: I'd really like to talk about politics, if everybody's willing, I suggested.

Meridel laughed. There you go again, separating things, dividing them up into proper little categories, she accused. She gave me a warm hug and turned to greet her friends. We all drifted slowly into the living room and settled comfortably down to our "discussion."

Bill leaned back carefully. I know the idea of the collective is central to your political beliefs, Meridel, but I don't know how I feel down deep about collectives, he mused. You know, there's this idea of "first right" or "first reeve" that I keep coming back to when I think about my own work with other people. Let's say, for example, that I went out of the collective and harvested three or four bushels of tomatoes, and brought them back to the group. I would figure that the collective would give me the responsibility of distributing my work, and have faith enough that I would share the tomatoes with them. If they wanted to go through the basket later and re-evaluate the choices I made, that would be all right, but it seems that there's something unfair if I pick the tomatoes and then everyone else digs in on an equal basis. It's like the community didn't respect the labor of the first reeve, the right to first judgment.

Meridel: Well, I don't think the fact that they dived in and took the tomatoes would deny your work or the fact that they appreciated your contribution. There's a different kind of recognition in a collective than is in bourgeois society. You're not a hero because you're good in the dance, or because you put everything you have into the dance. You have to have confidence that the process will continue without any ego gratification in it. Like Pauline Olivaris' music. She has confidence that there is a tone in which we all exist and if we all make our own tone, the tone that will emerge will be amazing, beautiful, and something in which we can all resonate. We don't have this confidence in the communal tone — we don't even share it with nature and the cosmos. You can see your work differently, if you understand it in light of this consciousness. Your work is marvelous because it complements others' labors. (L).

Neala: But Meridel, isn't there some kind of conflict inherent in what you're saying? Like in the women's movement today. We've all been repressed and oppressed for so long, and now we hear each other saying for the first time, "yes, you're wonderful, you're important, you're a marvelous individual and your contribution is unique to your own, feminine experience." But what happens if I'm in a collective of all men? Like "reality?" What if I speak from my heart, my center, and they tell me that I see the world wrong — that I have to see it the male way. What if the "dance" is a male dance, a dance that contradicts my individual, feminine perceptions and beliefs?

M: But then it wouldn't be a true collective, don't you see? They would quickly come to see that their actions were not communal or collective, because they weren't listening to *your* voice. I don't think you can have a real trust and openness between people unless you're part of a body, unless you have a consciousness of the whole and your relationship with it. If you're just individuals, you can't trust each other. The crucial problem in a collective society is trust. You have to learn to trust the commune. You can't compete with each other. If it was a true collective you would use each other's differences and they would become a strength for the collective.

N: From my own experiences with collectives this past couple of years, I still have some doubts about collective work in general. There were times when we just sort of floundered around, with no direction. The great pooling of knowledge and insights were often lost in the hassle of getting some of the simplest things done. I guess like Bill here, I have trouble with the "how and when" to decide who's

going to be in charge of, or perhaps responsible for, getting
something done.

M: I don't believe in leaders, she interrupted. If you're
going to be a leader then you're responsible, and you're
responsible for the good as well as the bad. All that rests
on one person, what that individual thinks is right (T9).

N: Well, then, if not a leader what about a director,
someone to organize things, you know, not authoritarian,
but taking responsibility and making decisions so that
things will go more smoothly and quickly?

M: If you don't trust the body, they they you've got to have a
director. You don't need leaders or directors — the
collective must become skilled as a whole. When you're
not skilled, there will be a weakness (T9).

N: Maybe that's what I'm trying to sort out — skills. What
if someone else has better skills than I do at certain things?
Like in the film collective. One woman said that even if
none of us knew how to run a camera we could do it
anyway, because, as the song goes, "you can be anything
you want to be." But that's denying that some women know
more about cameras, are better photographers, or have had
years of training or wider experiences. I'm for honoring
that in some way.

M: There you go, saying it again, she replied impatiently.
You don't say "better." Everyone has certain things to
contribute to the collective, but that doesn't make them a
leader. That makes them — like if you have a good liver
and a good kidney. They both have to be good in order to
make a good body. That kidney isn't a "leader" because
it's a damn good kidney. It's not going to take over the
function of the liver! They're both necessary. If the
kidney says, "Oh, God, I'm wonderful — I'm going to take
it away from the liver," why then you've got kidney stones
(T9).

N: But that's what I'm saying! I can't be both. I can write,
but maybe I can't run a camera.

M: So who wants you to be! But you don't have to be an authority on writing, either. Authority is a dangerous concept to collective pi ocesses. Look at the intellectuals. Somebody's an "authority" or an "expert." That draws everything in one direction for a while, like the Southern Agrarians did in the Thirties. Ruins the collective, poisons the intellectual climate, because they've used their skills to become "authorities" (T9).

N: What about a theory that many anarchists have — a belief in the spontaneous leader — someone who emerges in a moment of disaster or crisis and organizes the people, serves as a sort of temporary leader?

M: Yes, and he does it. The body works in that way, too, against disease. But there is still a danger in leaders. In Guatemala during the earthquakes recently, all the authorities came in with their bulldozers and big equipment to clear away the rubble. But the people laid down in front of the bulldozers, saying "don't knock down our stones. We're going to build on that base like we've done for thousands of years." There are times when the collective knowledge has to fight authority. All those "expert" scientists with their great minds couldn't stop the atomic bomb. They weren't part of the body of the people, they couldn't mobilize the rest of the body to help them stop it. (T9).

Don: I think there's another way of looking at leadership, besides the "crisis" orientation. Generally things can be done collectively and decisions made within the collective. At times decisions need to be made elsewhere and delegates can be instructed how to represent the collective. This is the method of anarcho-syndicalism and federation from below. The best example was the CNT[28] (Confederacion Nacional del Trabajo) in Spain during the Thirties. Even with hundreds of thousands of members, all questions were discussed before national gatherings... There is a danger in relying on "crisis" leadership — this is what led to the strengthening of the American presidency, especially during and since World War II. The "necessity" of crisis leadership is also put forward as the way to solve current ecological, energy and other crises by pessimists like Robert Hailbroner. It's the old "man on the white horse" syndrome — the man who will "save" us.[29]

N: But what about special skills? Like your writing, Meridel. That's not something you can do collectively. It's unique and individual, isn't it?

M: Skills are to be given to the collective. There's no such thing as a skill to be an authority. If you're a great poet, you're not given anything by being a great poet, you're a great poet because you can give the people this great vision, but you're not an authority because you can write great poetry. People don't bow down to you. When you have become a conduit for tremendous beautiful visions, and you're honored as a person who gives to the community, you have raised the level of the whole community and that's a different thing. As Mao says, you must remember that the littlest person has an important vision. When you're sitting in the circle, you wait for hours and hours and wait until the mute and dumb person shows that he's seeing something very important to the commune. He may have a vision which might unlock the whole knowledge of the commune. Everyone is of equal importance. You need the contributions of everyone — wait all night if you have to. You don't do away with skills, you give them to the commune. You don't give it with authority, and say "I'm right." You meet until everyone agrees — wait for the consensus. You meet until everyone has the same vision. No one is ever defeated. You never take a vote (T9).

N: In our collective there were a lot of individual egos operating — my own included. It's a long way from theory to practice. My family, which is a kind of commune, has the same problems. Sometimes I confess that just being the mother and giving orders and making decisions is the only way that things get done. At times it seems pretty idealistic to keep meeting until everybody sees the same vision. Sometimes we're at each other's throats — all with separate visions of what the "right" way is — alternately trying to sway each other with friendly persuasion — all trying to have our vision be the dominant one. What if it takes a whole year to get the whole group to agree on a vision? And then, even though we would struggle collectively, there would always be that majority rule at the end — and I often felt tyrannized by that majority. But no one got upset when he/she was in the majority!

Bill: That's a good point. Does the collective get as angry about the tyranny of the majority as it does about the individual ego?

N: De Tocqueville warned us a long time ago that one of the inherent weaknesses in democracy was just that tendency to reduce everything to the lowest common denominator. Like diluting an idea until there's nothing left of it. And the way that the majority can most easily tyrannize is to "guilt-trip" the individual. The worst thing anyone can say in a collective is that you're on an ego trip. Shuts you right up!

M: That's where trust comes in again. Trust that the others will listen to your vision. In a true collective you would contribute to the others whatever you thought was necessary. We are in a historic time now of imperfect people trying to form a collective. Of course you're going to have a lot of ego problem initially! What I think we all have to recognize is that the leadership ego is the biggest threat to the collective. And it's a hard thing for all of us. Brought up as we are to excel and to want to succeed. The idea of hierarchy is a dangerous thing. If you have to look up to someone, or demand recognition for yourself from another person, your growth is stifled. You always see yourself below that other person, or her below you. This destroys the collective. When you deify someone, make them larger than they are, you don't grow, and neither do they.

N: My own experience in hierarchies taught me something else, too. If you're on the bottom, you have no way of expressing your potential. You are stuck with having only a small part, a piece of something, never knowing how it relates to the whole. If you're in the hierarchy near the top, you have the opposite problem. You can, theoretically, self-actualize, but one person can't do it all! You see all the weight thrust on your shoulders and no way of getting it accomplished in a situation where you need the help of others, but they are hostile to your authority.

Mary: When we lived in Minneapolis, everyone thought you were larger than life there, Meridel. I remember there was a time years back when you were in a crummy space for some reason. Everyone talked about it, but nobody would go to you saying, "what the hell is wrong, Meridel?" or "why are you so weird, Meridel, what's going on?" Nobody would level with you.

M: Well none of you trusted me! In a collective you have to trust that a person's not going to say, "I don't like you when you're this way" in order to kill you or destroy you. You're not saying something to me hampered sharing and communication. I was crummy because I thought you all were crummy! And when I was in Minneapolis, I didn't feel larger than life. I felt like a mouse — I felt injured and abandoned. That's a bourgeois hangover — creating those kinds of larger than life people.

Don: Maybe we ought to make a distinction between heroines and "models." Since many inspirations and acts are done at first by one or two or a few people, we might be able to look at their actions and say, "Yes, that's a good thing to do," or "that's what I would have done in the same situation." It's putting the hero or heroine as abstract and above that's bad. If it's something that everyone can do and relate to and find analogous to their own situation, what's wrong with that? My pottery instructor once said that we

*are all influenced by others, but we each have to digest that
influence, i.e., run it through our brain or heart or
whatever.*[30]

M: So now you see the dangers of the hierarchy. The
concept of conquest is at the base of this idea of hierarchy.
That's racism. You make another race foul, dirty, terrible, and most importantly, inferior. Then you conquer
them. In a collective you wouldn't have this concept of
power and conquest, the imbalance. Philosophers have
helped the conquerors by their philosophies of objectivity
and alienation and mechanism. But in a collective this
linear philosophy of cause and effect is no longer true.
Cause and effect is a male linear ploy, invented by the
scientific world to make everything maneuverable,
conquerable, knowable. It's outside of you — you have no
responsibility to it.

But in the collective, if you know that everything you
do is going to affect the cosmos because it's all connected,
you have a marvelous new understanding of responsibility. It's like the Indian Sun Dance that I go to.
They say that every person affects the sun and has
responsibility to the sun. This is true. Suppose you felt
responsible to the sun? That would be connected. And in
love (T15).

The potentials and the revelations of oppression are
being exposed like they never were in the world before.
Sometimes I have the feeling that the future is almost
like alchemy, like magic, because there are so many
things being released — in science and human relationship and communality and social structures and social
organization. A whole new kind of concept seems to me to
be coming up in people of how to be together or how to
organize society, or how to oppose death and destruction
and dissection and massacre. There isn't hardly anybody
that doesn't know the destructiveness of the establishment, and it seems to me that that makes a new world
almost inevitable (Film Outtakes).

From Theory to Practice

Anarchists have always demanded the integration of theory and direct political action. For Le Sueur, too, involvement in radical politics was not limited to merely recording or interpreting the actions around her. Through her long years of dedication and commitment to radical political work, we can document literally hundreds of demonstrations in which she took part, rallies she attended, meetings she chaired, events at which she read her work to raise funds. Through her many years of activism, she never ran for public office, or vied for power in small groups. *How* she was politically active is a reflection of her beliefs — an extension of her ideology into practice. Always encouraging decentralization, grass roots activism, consensus decision-making, collective action — Le Sueur helped bring a new sensitivity to midwestern political radicals.

She has taken her message of freedom and equality to people in every conceivable manner, lending her energies to anti-war movements, anarchists, communists, socialists, feminists, artists — radicals of every persuasion who advance the cause of the people. She has spent her life talking with people, being among people, sharing their pain and understanding their oppression. She has marched on picket lines protesting the execution of Sacco and Vanzetti or the presence of the FBI on Indian Reservations; worked in communal kitchens during the 1934 Trucker's Strike in Minneapolis; organized for the Communist Party; celebrated nourishing the earth; and encouraged young poets and artists — all with the personal touch of gossiping over the backyard fence on a warm summer evening. There is no meaningless conversation for Le Sueur —always she speaks for the social and political struggle — to fight oppression, to love the land, to work collectively to be free.

Meridel grounds her political theories in this radical

tradition of the American Marxist-anarchist and focuses much of her criticism against exploitation and oppression. At the same time, she has avoided a formalist, dogmatist position. Her daughter, Deborah, recalled times when Meridel was asked to speak at meetings or political rallies, that she was asked to "tone down" her style — not to speak so passionately, so directly and intimately. Her lyricism and passion in a warm, open, all-embracing political theory — liberally sprinkled with bodily metaphors — make most Puritanical people uneasy — even if they were Communists! Part of the difficulty may have lain in the expansive and broad interpretation of oppression that Meridel taught. In her writing and speaking, oppression was not limited to economic factors; it was endemic in all facets of capitalistic culture — from racism and sexism, to literary criticism. Every act was a political act; and in order to be truly revolutionary, the analysis had to extend beyond the economic.

> I don't disassociate politics from being able to eat, or live or love. I hate that thing that politics is something "special." Politics is the way that you associate with power, I think — your relationship to power and how you feel about power. I never made any divisions like that. The struggle to live, and to get food, and not to be crushed or run over by the power structure — that's politics to me. Keep your children alive, and all other children alive, and at least somewhat free not to be smashed, in their hearts and minds (T3).

The Art of Politics

Lastly, the aesthetic dimension of anarchism deserves exploration. In the tradition of anarchist thought, artists and the artistic have long been embraced — both analogously and metaphorically — as philosophical sisters. Anarchists, more than any other political theoreticians have always paid homage to the aesthetic as an integral part of the "political" self. A tradition of "people's art" moves beyond the mere realism of Marxism to the appreciation of the depth of the creative force driving human life. Aesthetics, then, becomes the *elan vital* or the celebration of the joy of being — since the truly free person, anarchists believe, will celebrate the creative force. Anarchist political activism, too, has long encouraged the spontaneous "act" — an act of theatrical significance in many ways. We need only recall the "yippies" of our own time to appreciate the fun and spontaneity anarchism embraces. Street theater, the significant flambouyant act (which does not become institutionalized), the wry sense of humor so lacking in marxists for example — all spring from the anarchist aesthetic sense. As we are aware, the more organic world views tend to be based, in part, on just such an aesthetic apprehension. The *gestalt* of Paul Goodman's psychology resembles the spontaneous direct political action so dear to anarchists. Ultimately, anarchism celebrates the richness of this human and environmental existence — and the aesthetic underlying it generates the spirit of a revolutionary culture.

For Meridel, art was always a political act. The aesthetic apprehension of our whole political reality affords an integrated understanding of the relationships which serve to maintain an oppressive reality. At the same time, it is this holistic apprehension which allows us to act upon and change our political reality in an aesthetic way. It is only when we "see" in this integrated way, that we can truly act politically. And that "seeing" is an aesthetic sense, a need for making connections and seeing relationships. It allows for inclusiveness, the embracing of apparent contradictions, which are the foundations of a dialectical understanding and the secret to understanding the essence of collectivity. It is the celebration of those patterns reflecting the underlying spirit of a truly revolutionary culture.

Writing was always Meridel's primary political activity, and her style reflects a unique interweaving of politics-history-poetry. This aesthetic apprehension of the integrity of the world is a unique aspect of anarchist thought which is often overlooked. It allows for that inclusiveness, that embracing of apparent contradictions which, in reality, are the foundations of a dialectical understanding. Ultimately, it is the celebration of the richness of our human existence — those patterns reflecting the underlying spirit of a truly revolutionary culture.

Many of Le Sueur's stories recount specific political actions
and activities of people struggling to make changes in their
lives. "What Happens in a Strike" (a story about the 1934
Trucker's Strike in Minneapolis), "A Hungry Intellectual" (a
devastating description of a man unable to make a commitment, although he was "intellectually" aware of the conflicts
within the culture), "I Was Marching!" (again, portraying the
Trucker's Strike and the necessity for human solidarity),
"Murder In Minneapolis" (a drama of strikers killed at the
Flour City Architectural Metals Company), and "Minneapolis
Counts Its Victims," again recounting political actions.

In other stories she documented direct exploitation and
even murder. "Iron Country" was an expose' of the mining
companies of the Mesabi Range who fired workers they found
suffering from lung diseases; "The Derned Crick's Rose,"
illuminating Marx's theory of the alienation of workers from
the means of production; and "The Dead in Steel" showed the
courage and heroism of union organizers and their families.
Other stories detailed the devastation of the drought in the
Midwest: "Cows and Horses are Hungry," "Tonight is Part of
the Struggle," "Salute to Spring," "The Farmers Face a
Crisis," and "How Drought Relief Works." War, too, was
examined from the viewpoint of victims and families in stories
like "Song for my Time," "Breathe Upon These Slain," and
"The Way It Seems." Over and over, from countless perspectives, Meridel pointed out the real enemy of American
democracy, the real enemy of the hungry:

> Now from city to city the real source of violence in American life was
> naked — the violence of corporate wealth able to starve you, control
> your jobs, your life, your being. This is the true violence. When people
> tell you that violence comes from the streets or from the unemployed or
> from the Third World, this is not true. The real violence is the hunger
> and the speculation and the destruction of the crops of the people. This is
> the real terror of our time (Film).

As the drought and depression deepened in the midwest,
people organized in Unemployed Councils and the Worker's
Alliance, taking to the streets with their issues, demanding
work and a decent life. Many of Meridel's activities centered

around a community of writers and artists who lived near downtown St. Paul "where the rent was cheap." Many artists were involved in the WPA Writers' Project — teaching, painting, working together in theater collectives and writing communes. As part of their WPA work, they published state Guides and wrote histories of every county in Minnesota. Meridel published *Worker Writer* during these years — a technical writing manual which she used in her writing classes.

Life in the depression was not all political meetings. These years, although harsh, are remembered by Meridel and her friends with great warmth.

> It really was a great community. And the artists really did work for the workers. The Worker's Alliance was an organization of unemployed workers and unemployed artists. This was a tremendous cultural thing. Whenever workers organize anything they naturally have poetry and music. The IWW's used to say that every worker was a poet, and the only poets were workers and that you had a right to sing your song (T5).

> She raised her children by herself. Made that commitment to raise her family alone. It was a courage thing in those days. I remember going to Loring Park with her and the children where a woman threatened to have Meridel arrested because she had a naked baby in the park!
> We went on picnics. I never thought you could have a picnic with a whole carrot and a whole tomato — or just take a green pepper out and eat it. The simplest things in life were such a revelation to me being with Meridel. They led to big freedom in my life (T17).

The Minnesota Left took a strong interest in the struggles for democracy in Spain during the Thirties, sending a brigade from Minnesota to fight Franco. With the coming of the Second World War, most members of the Communist Party supported the fight against Hitler and Fascism. Much political energy during those war years was directed at a national effort to establish a Second Front in an effort to aid the beseiged Russian people. In Minnesota, the Farmer-Labor Party was in the throes of a power struggle between the Leftist founders of the party and the more conservative faction led by Humbert Humphrey, Orville Freeman and Eugenie Anderson. All of these events, however, were overshadowed by the dropping of the first atomic bomb. Meridel recalled her response:

In 1945 the first atomic bomb was dropped on Hiroshima and then Nagasaki with no warning. Dropped by Truman who said he never lost a night's sleep over it — and by the democratic country of America.

My daughter said she heard of it in school, and she ran home glad that the war was over. She entered a darkened house. Her mother and grandmother were sitting and mourning in the dark, the curtains drawn.

They said this is the end of an era. This is the end of America as we have known it. This is a terrible thing for the human (Journals).

In the years following the end of the war, Minnesota radicals devoted their energy to building the Progressive Party and the election of Henry Wallace. But the mood of the country had changed and the ensuing McCarthy Era would destroy many movements and injure many personal lives, Meridel's included. The reign of terror was focused initially on the arts — ironic since just the decade before the debate had been settled that art and politics were separate!

I was surrounded, lassooed. It was impossible to make a living, to get a job as a waitress. A week, and the boss would say, I'm sorry, the FBI was here. My classes in writing were closed down. I had a correspondence course to try and live and every enrolled student across the U.S. was intimidated, threatened, and had to drop out. The McCarthy period. That attack upon the people in the Hitler pattern. Fascism was not dead. It had taken new forms. Our house was bugged, two FBI agents sat outside day and night. The phone was tapped (Journals).

Despite the repression, Meridel continued her writing and speaking. She edited *The People Together*, a people's history of Minnesota's first 100 years; visited people in prison; teaching when she could; struggling to keep the boarding house in Kenwood afloat. A forerunner of today's communes, the house operated on a pay-when-you-can basis, and everyone was welcomed: "She let people live there for little or no rent — paying what they could. She didn't always have money to keep it up or fulfill the requirements of all the city ordinances. The FBI harrassed her out of the house — every day an inspector would come."(T17).

During the 50's, she turned to writing children's books. Even here, however, she was subject to bitter criticism and attacks on her politics. In 1954, the Milwaukee Sentinel published a particularly vicious critique. With headlines reading "Red Party Line is Catch Line in New Abe Lincoln

Book," the article continued:

> The trouble is that you can't just relax and enjoy it, you have to stay up on your toes and watch the curves. The unforgettable thing about the producers of communist art is that no matter how good they are as artists they have to use their art to push the message, otherwise known as the party line... One suggestion is that religion is a myth and the other is that Abe Lincoln's society was divided into two hostile classes: a minority of rich people and a vast mass of oppressed workers and farmers. Oddly enough these two ideas illustrate two of the cardinal ideas of the CP line: aesthetic materialism and the necessity of class struggle... This finally is a book to be read carefully and in company with other books if at all. No youngster should be allowed to trap himself into thinking it is the whole story of Abraham Lincoln.[31]
>
> Frankly we think an old hand like Meridel Le Sueur is an unfair match for a youngster at least until they have had a few workouts in the manly art of intellectual self-defense. After that we can trust them to go the distance with Meridel any day. Now we don't particularly favor burning Meridel's books in the court of honor, but we think it should be restricted for use in some way, perhaps through the schools, so that it will be read only in context with other books about Abe Lincoln (and early Americans) which approach the problem from a traditional American viewpoint.[32]

A recent spate of books and television specials have broadened our understanding of the terror and Fascism of the McCarthy Era, but we have yet to grasp the "why" of our national hysteria. Even more importantly, we need to understand the personal agonies of those members of the radical community who were forced underground and who's life work was attacked and destroyed in that witchhunt. The madness and terror of the time will be a long time healing before we understand the damage done to American culture. It is an era which Meridel finds especially difficult to discuss — perhaps because the pain was so deeply felt.

Although it was a difficult time personally for Meridel, she refused then and still refuses, to remember those years as a personal disaster. Her writing was never completely silenced, and while her song reached fewer ears, her courage and strength were a powerful inspiration for many people. With a clear voice and a proud community around her, she refused to allow her vision to be altered or smashed. In a firm voice she continued to point out the enemy:

> Our people in America are in deep anguish. They are in the dark of

Capitalism. The assassin passes through your hands daily as the product you make passes into the chaos of a market you never know. The people suffer under Capitalism in a different way than a colonial people, for the masks are cunning and the naked wars of aggression are hidden under the words of democracy, and you are delivered into the death of wars against people you do not hate, and made guilty by Nagasakis and Hiroshimas you did not plan (DT, 12).

Her faith never flagged, and in the years which followed Meridel continued to teach, write and support the struggle of oppressed people. The song of the radical American now reached from the democratic villages of the midwest to her brothers and sisters in villages around the world:

The Village has always lain in the path of the conqueror. The villages of Viet Nam, of Africa, of Peru and Brazil, of Ireland, Spain, Mexico, Cuba, Haiti, Iowa, New Mexico, Thailand, look up in anger at the sky filled with fire, at napalm burning crops and skin, and still they plunder the Village and the Villagers.

Name Lidice, the villages of pogroms, Guernica; from the Big Horn to Viet Nam — the Massacre of Wounded Knee to the Mekong Delta, the same Village — our Village (RAR, 45).

One final note: Meridel will take exception to my interpretation of her as an anarchist — or any other label, for that matter. In one sense she is right. The essence of anarchism seems to be something that transcends deliberate analysis. In all its myriad explications it expresses something beyond ideology, some great hope and firm belief that can appear in many forms — political, aesthetic, even religious at times. For all its limitations, however, anarchist theory represents something profoundly creative and life-affirming — the voice of human conscience.

ENDNOTES

[1] J.R. Conlin, *Bread and Roses, Too* (Westport, Conn.: Greenwood Publishing Corp., 1969), p. 82.

[2] Emma Goldman, *Living My Life* (New York: Dover Publications, 1970) p. 408.

[3] A. Landy, *Marxism and the Democratic Tradition* (New York: International Publishers, 1946), p. 161.

[4] See Daniel Aaron, *Writers on the Left* (New York: Avon Books, 1961), Henry Hart, Ed., *American Writers' Congress* (New York: International Publishers, 1935), Granville Hicks, et. al., *Proletarian Literature in the United States* (New York: International Publishers, 1935), Richard H. Pellis, *Radical Visions and American Dreams* (New York: Harper & Row, 1973), and others.

[5] There are many good general studies of midwestern radical thought. See Arne Hallonen, "The Role of Finnish Americans in the Political Labor Movement," University of Minnesota, Unpublished Masters Thesis, 1948: John D. Hicks, *The Populist Revolt — A History of the Farmers Alliance and the People's Party* (Lincoln, Nebraska: University of Nebraska Press, 1961); Robert L. Morland, *Political Prairie Fire: The Non-Partisan League 1915-1922* (Minneapolis: University of Minnesota Press, 1955); John Wefald, *A Voice of Protest: Norwegians in American Politics 1890-1917* (Northfield, Minnesota: Norwegian-American Historical Association, 1971); James M. Youngdale, *Populism: A Psychohistorical Perspective* (Port Washington, N.Y.: Kennikat Press, 1975); James M. Youngdale, Ed. *Third Party Footprints: An Anthology from Writings and Speeches of Midwest Radicals* (Minneapolis: Ross & Haines, Inc., 1966).

[6] David DeLeon, *The American As Anarchist* (Baltimore and London: Johns Hopkins University Press, 1978).

[7] A.E. Zucker, Ed., *The Forty Eighters: Political Refugees of the German Revolution* (New York: Columbia University Press, 1950).

[8] See William H. Goetzman, *The American Hegelians: An Intellectual Episode in the History of Western America* (New York: A.A. Knopf, 1973); Charles M. Perry, *The St. Louis Movement in Philosophy* (Norman, Oklahoma: University of Oklahoma Press, 1930); Paul R. Anderson, *Platonism in the Midwest* (New York: Columbia University Press, 1963); Carl Wittke, *The Utopian Communist: A Biography of Wilhelm Weitling, Nineteenth Century Reformer* (Baton Rouge, Louisiana: Louisiana State University Press, 1950); J. Gabriel Woerner, *The Rebel's Daughter* (Boston: Little, Brown, 1899); and others.

[9] There are many studies of the IWW or Wobblies: Paul F. Brissenden, *The IWW: A Study of American Syndicalism* (New York: Columbia University Press, 1920); J.R. Conlin, *Bread and Roses, Too: Studies of the Wobblies* (Westport, Connecticut: Greenwood Publishing Corp., 1969); Melvyn Dubofsky, *We Shall Be All: A History of the IWW* (New York: New York Times Book Co., 1969); William Haywood, *Bill Haywood's Book* (New York: International Publishers, 1929); Patrick Renshaw, *The Wobblies: The Story of Syndicalism in the United States* (Garden City, N.Y.: Doubleday, 1967); Philip Taft, "The IWW in the Grain Belt," (*Labor History*, 1, 1960 pp. 53-67); Robert L. Tyler, "The IWW and the West," in Hennig Cohen, Ed., *The American Culture* (Boston: Houghton Mifflin, 1968).

[10] See Hyman Berman, "Education for Work and Labor Solidarity: The Immigrant Miners and Radicalism on the Mesabi Range," Unpublished article in the Minnesota Historical Society Collection; Neil Betten, "Strike on the Mesabi - 1907," (*Minnesota History*, (1967), pp. 340-347); Neil Betten, "Riot, Repression in the Iron Range Strike of 1916," (*Minnesota History*, 41 (1968), pp. 82-93); Many nationally-known radicals came to the Range: Emma Goldman was in St. Paul in 1907, Elizabeth Gurley Flynn, Mother Jones and Mother Bloor, esp.

[11] Early midwestern pacifist tendencies reflect both a philosophical commitment to peace and a distrust of centralized authority. Although Minnesotans — especially the Germans — were among the first groups to fight in the Civil War, they were strongly anti-war by the time of World War I. Arguments against this war were partly isolationist and partly "political" — in that war was seen as fights between monarchies, and not peoples.

[12] In the Anti-Saloon League of the early 20th Century, we find an interesting mix of women's politics and anti-immigrant, anti-radical sentiment. The argument has been made that the Prohibition Movement was a movement to destroy an institution (the tavern) central to working-class society.

[13] See Hicks, *op. cit.*, Richard Hofstadter, *The Age of Reform* (New York: Random House, 1955), and Youngdale, *populism op. cit.*

[14] In 1851, the Turner national association published the following definition of socialism: "Socialism of today, in which we Turners believe, aims to remove the pernicious antagonism between labor and capital. It endeavors to effect a reconciliation between these two,

and to establish a peace by which the rights of the former are fully protected against the encroachments of the latter. . . However, since self-preservation is the inherent impulse of the human race, the ultimate solution of this vital problem will be in the final victory of the oppressed classes. They, in their turn, must not violate justice in their demands. They must not endeavor to build up some sort of a new aristocracy of the working class upon the ruins of the old aristocratic class, with its manifold privileges and numerous monopolies and its unwarrantable advantages — an heritage bestowed by the blind accident of birth. We wish all men to be working men, sustaining themselves by the produce of their labor, but by no means do we favor the creation of new class distinctions upon the overthrow of the present ruling class." In Zucker, *op. cit.*

[15] Many of Le Sueur's works are now being reprinted: *Song for My Time, Harvest, Women on the Breadlines,* (1977) and her novel, *The Girl,* (1978), have all been published by West End Press. International Publishers has reprinted their 1940 collection of her stories, *Salute to Spring* (1977) and Feminist Press has a collection *Ripenings* in print (1982). Still out of print is the bulk of her work, including *Corn Village* (Sauk City, Wis.: Stanton & Lee, 1970), *Crusaders,* op. cit., *North Star Country* (a history of the upper midwest), (New York: Duell Sloan & Pearce, 1945), and several children's books. A recent collection of poetry, *Rites of Ancient Ripening,* has been released by Vanilla Press of Minneapolis (1975, 1976).

[16] Again, many resources for Indian philosophies. See, especially, A. Chapman, Ed., *Literature of the American Indian* (New York: New American Library, 1974); Lame Deer (John Fire) and Richard Erdoes, *Lame Deer: Seeker of Visions* (New York: Simon & Schuster, 1972); Neihardt, John C., *Black Elk Speaks* (Lincoln, Nebraska: University of Nebraska Press, 1961); *The Writer's Sense of Place: A symposium and Commentaries* (*South Dakota Review,* 13, 3, Autumn, 1975); Jamake Highwater, *The Primal Mind* (New York: Harper & Row, 1981) Russell Means, "Native American Spiritual Values," April 4, 1974, Radio Address, Minnesota Public Radio, Audio Archive No. 116; Hyemeyohsts Storm, *Seven Arrows* (New York: Ballantine Books, 1972); George F. Will and George E. Hyde, *Corn Among the Indians of the Upper Missouri* (Lincoln, Neb.: University of Nebraska Press, 1917, Reprtd, 1964); Vina Deloria, Jr., *God Is Red* (New York: Dell Publishing, 1973), and many others.

[17] Lame Deer, *op. cit.,* p. 128.

[18] Paula Gunn Allen, "The Sacred Hoop," in Chapman, *op. cit.,* p. 128.

[19] Max Stirner, *The Ego and Its Own: The Case of the Individual Against Authority* (New York: Dover Publications, Inc., reprinted 1845, 1963, 1973), p. 250.

[20] For a brief, but insightful analysis of this particular issue, see a new pamphlet entitled "Disease" put out by Falling Sky Books, 97 Victoria Street North, Kitchener, Ontario, Canada N2H5C1, which includes an excerpt of *Apocalisse a Rivoluzione,* by Gianni Collu and Giorgio Cesarano (1973), two Italian anarchist theorists. Entitled "Transitions," the article states: "This transition is a movement from value as an abstract quantity arising out of the production of goods to value as an objectified thing in itself, for the sake of which all goods are produced, and in respect to which all human activities are judged." (p. 19). Basically, the article expands the idea of value itself as it emerges from the practice of capitalism: "Capital as a social mode of production realizes its own real domination when it comes to substitute all the social or natural presuppositions that existed before it with organizational forms, specifically of its own, that mediate the submission of all physical and social life to its own valorization needs; the essence of the "Gemeinschaft" of capital is realized as organization. (pp. 21-22)
See also Peter Berger, et. al., *The Homeless Mind: Modernization* and *Consciousness* (New York: Vintage Books, 1973) for a description of what Berger calls "functional rationality" which is imposed on our political, social and personal lives by the economy of technology. Also, chapter on "Ownership" in E.F. Schumacher, *Small is Beautiful* (New York: Harper & Row, 1973).

[21] Stirner, p. 251.

[22] Stirner, p. 258.

[23] Meridel Le Sueur, letter to Neala Schleuning, received January 13, 1976.

[24] Emma Goldman, "The Tragedy of Women's Emancipation," in Alix Kates Shulman, ed., *Red Emma Speaks: Selected Writings and Speeches by Emma Goldman* (New York: Vintage Books, 1973).

[25] It is on the question of decentralization that anarchists and communists have traditionally parted company. I base my analysis of Le Sueur's philosophy on this distinction. Although she worked for many years with the Communist party, an examination of both private and public documents written by Le Sueur failed to indicate any commitment to centralization of power.

[26] Irene Paull, letter to me, received April, 1976.

[27] The bulk of this dialogue was recorded in a conversation between Meridel, and Mary and Bill Maxine, July, 1976. These comments are not footnoted. This dialogue is structured from a variety of sources: published writings, unpublished works, letters, personal conversations, lectures, tapes, interview with friends, etc. The particular discussions presented never actually took place as self contained units.

[28] Murray Bookchin, "The Forms of Freedom," *Post Scarity Anarchism*, pp. 153-154. "Perhaps the only instance where a system of working-class self-management succeeded as a mode of *class* organization was in Spain, where anarchosyndicalism attracted a large number of workers and peasants to its banner. The Spanish anarcho-syndicalists *consciously* sought to limit the tendency toward centralization. The CNT (Confederacion Nacional del Trabajo), the large anarchosyndicalist union in Spain, created a dual organization with an elected committee system to act as a control on local bodies and national congresses. The assemblies had the power to revoke their delegates to the council and countermand council decisions. For all practical purposes the "higher" bodies of the CNT functions as coordinating bodies. Let there be no mistake about the effectiveness of this scheme of organization; it imparted to each member of the CNT a weighty sense of responsibility, a sense of direct, immediate and personal influence in the activities and politics of the union. This responsibility was exercised with a highminded-ness that made the CNT the most militant as well as the largest revolutionary movement in Europe during the interwar decades."

[29] Don Olson, Letter. Randolph Bourne was also troubled by the tendency to idealize individuals. "(T)he way in which our society does do honor to its indubitably great and serviceable men... is a study in immunizing people against their virus... They are transformed into striking images and personalities, as we assign to them the Role of being great men... This effectually prevents the two practical uses that we could make of them. We neither take seriously the simple, direct, fearless souls that they inevitably are, whther humble or arrogant, to model ourselves after them because they make more sense as human beings; nor do we have recourse to them please to help us when we have need of exceptional purity, magnanimity, profundity, or imagination, giving them a free hand on the assumption that their action is really better. Though we publicize the image, we do not behave as though we really believed that there were great men, a risky fact in the world... I understand that to consider powerful souls as if they were a useful public resource is quite foreign to our customs. In a small sense it is undemocratic, for it assumes that some people really know better in a way that must seem arbitrary to most. In a large sense it is certainly democratic, in that it makes the great man serve as a man. Either of these choices... is preferable to creating glamorous images with empty roles." Bourne, pp. 152-154.

[31] Milwaukee *Sentinel* (Milwaukee, Wis.), November 28, 1954.

[32] Book Review, Milwaukee *Sentinel* (Milwaukee, Wis.,), November 28, 1954.

"I Hope Some Lover of the Future
Can Decipher Me, I Truly Want to Leave
a Message on the Wall"

The Literary Left

Meridel's emergence as a writer in the Thirties paralleled a strong literary movement unique to American history — the Literary Left. It was the Depression and the political unrest of the Thirties that provided the most powerful stimulus for the development of this radical aesthetic. World War I had overburdened the American economy, and in the years following the weight of the debt fell on the American people. Once again, the American Dream had come on hard times. And once, again, radical politics seemed the answer. The revolution this time was an indigenous one. There was no Emma Goldman to deport.

Significantly, this "new" revolution began in the arts and it was the writers especially who responded to the call for social change and revolution. Much of the early energy and impetus for political and cultural transformation came from the John Reed Clubs, the artistic branch of the Communist Party. Seeking new ways to look at American culture, artists and writers turned their energies to developing a "proletarian" literature and a literary and aesthetic theory based on a working class analysis.

The attempt to formulate a new radical aesthetic was initiated at the First American Writers Congress in 1935. For the first time, American writers gathered to debate the role of art in American culture and to explore the relationship of art to politics. The debate among participants was often lively, and although they disagreed as to the nature of the true ideological perspective, they did come to agreement on some of the more basic principles of the new aesthetic.

One of the primary characteristics of the new aesthetic was that art was to be defined in "social" rather than formalistic terms. Art was not to be for art's sake, but art necessitated by the historical and social reality. This radical aesthetic was a challenge to WASP individualism — highlighting the profound differences between a social, communistic, collective ideology and one focusing on the subjective and private experiences of individuals. The radicals argued that a collective inspiration would produce not only different subject matter, but different modes of expression as well. The insistence on a sociological dimension to art would serve, Freeman[1] suggested, to ground the myths of the poet in reality. Cowley argued that the poet could not ignore politics, but should be wary of limiting ideologies:

> All poets are automatically revolutionary: if they are genuine poets. They exhibit every idea they handle at the moment of its disintegration. They are the perpetual foes of abstraction. What you demand is that

they reject the Capitalist abstractions and accept the Communist. By assuming the world a poet merely assumes that the present moment offers all the elements for a full statement of the human condition.[2]

Whatever their disagreements over the finer points of ideology, most participants at the Congress were committed to a "social" art form. In many ways, they merely echoed the words of an earlier spokesman for social art, Bill Haywood.

[Proletarian art would be] very much kindlier than your art. There will be a social spirit in it. Not so much boasting about personality. Artists won't be so egotistical. The highest ideal of an artist will be to write a song which the workers can sing, to compose a drama which great throngs of workers can perform out of doors. When we stop fighting each other — for wages of existence on one side, and for unnecessary luxury on the other — then perhaps we shall all become human beings and surprise ourselves with the beautiful things we do and make on the earth.[3]

Criticism of the Literary Left was aimed at two levels: the actual literary content and the politics which that content represented. While critics focused on "literary" criteria such as subject matter, conflicts between "rational" ideology and "fictional" art, and the lack of symbols in proletarian art, they also felt a need to criticize political ideology, particularly Communism. The Literary Left failed, these critics argued, because "real" art and "proletarian" art are mutually exclusive. "Real" art succeeds because it is not political.

Driven at times by an almost hysterical need to denounce this new form even as it struggled for expression, the critics also argued that art was "reflection" and not "action." It was an experience of the senses, not of the cognitive processes of human experience. This argument was initially articulated within the ranks of the Left itself, as a means of discrediting the more deterministic philosophies of the Marxists. The rigidity of Marxist determinism, according to *Partisan Review* advocates, precluded "true" art. The more deterministic the substance of art, the more it reverted to propaganda.

Its literary "line" stems from the understanding of Marxism as mechanical materialism. In philosophy, mechanical materialism assumes a direct determinism of the whole superstructure by the economic foundation, ignoring the dialectical interaction between consciousness and environment, and the reciprocal influence of the parts of the superstructure on each other and on the economic

> determinants. The literary counterpart of mechanical materialism faithfully reflects this vulgarization of Marxism. But its effects strike even deeper: it paralyzes the writer's capacities by creating a dualism between his artistic consciousness and his beliefs, thus making it impossible for him to achieve anything beyond fragmentary, marginal expression.[4]

While on the surface we might agree with this argument, the basis for it lay in the insistence on the separation of art and politics. It was not only determinism that Phillips and Rahv were obliged to criticize by taking this tack: it was also necessary to exclude politics *in toto* from the art form. Their ultimate conclusion was that proletarian writers were not "great" writers because they allowed the intrusion of politics into their art. Not only was it heresy, but it wasn't even "art." It was propaganda. The abstract quality of political ideas precluded their use in literature; and a literature which dealt with political questions was incapable of truly reflecting the complexities of the human spirit.

Other critics soon echoed this and other reservations. Irving Howe demanded that art and politics be separate; he argued that politics was a "violent intrusion" into the literary imagination. He echoed Phillips and Rahv in his insistence that art and politics had different subjects: "the novel tries to confront experience in its immediacy and closeness, while ideology is by its nature general and inclusive." Daniel Aaron suggested that the conversion to Marxism by many writers was a "defective romanticism." In rejecting the nature of social art, he argued that art could only be an individualistic process — that Communism is antithetical to the creative artist because it demands submission to the "group mind." [6] Aaron saw communism as a monolithic concept into which all writers of political realism were placed. Writers like Meridel who were closer to the monolith were rejected as "proletarian" writers. The writers who "escaped the deadly influence of Communism," are the "better" writers — those American literary figures who, while initially fascinated with the idea of revolution, ultimately came to see the error of their ways and returned to the true fold. Writers like Steinbeck, Dos Passos and Garland in particular moved from the Left to the extreme Right of the political spectrum. Aaron's final criticism of the proletarian writers was that they were out of touch with American realities. Revolution was not about to occur, and those who believed that it would were bankrupt in both their thinking and their art.

But as Pellis and others would argue, these critics generally were shouting into a vacuum. The Literary Left had had a remarkable impact on American art and aesthetic theory:

> In the early 1930s however, those who rejected proletarian literature were usually on the defensive. No matter how eloquently they celebrated the universality of art or the writer's dedication to this craft, they seemed unable to grasp that these ideals were simply less appealing to intellectuals at present than the desire to play a more direct role in American life. For most writers during the depression, the problem was not how to remain free but how to become committed.[7]

The new literature of the proletarian writers was, more than anything else, a literature of commitment and passionate involvement. They had taken to heart Christopher Caudwell's imperative:

> It is important to understand that art is no more propaganda than science. That does not mean that neither has a social role to perform. On the contrary, their role is one which is as it were primary to and more fundamental than that of propaganda: that of changing men's minds.[8]

A Dialectical Realism

In the midst of this great debate over the function of art, we find Meridel. She was a central figure on the Literary Left, engaging in many of the discussions and arguments concerning the role of literature in a revolutionary culture.

> On the question of art and politics. I think this is where Meridel is really a person of enormous depth and complexity. For years she was active with many of us in the Marxist movement. Some did not understand or like her literary work. You young women understand and like her work far better than the Marxists did. Our imaginations were stifled in the interests of immediate propaganda...
>
> Anyway, Meridel did the agit-prop work that was needed all through the Thirties and Forties and into the Fifties, but at the same time she maintained her literary integrity with what she wrote in her notebooks. She also found art in the struggle.
>
> Art and politics is a big subject. And there is no cut-and-dried answer. Sometimes art makes bad politics. Sometimes politics makes

bad art. Sometimes there is a marriage of the two that makes both great art and great politics.[9]

Meridel is an interesting figure in American literature because she was roundly criticized during the Thirties by both "sides." One recent anthologizer[10] remarked that "her early promise" as a writer was destroyed when she became "political." Segments of the Left felt she was too lyrical and passionate in her style — that she didn't conform to the party line. The editors of *New Masses*, for example, felt she portrayed the people in a depressing manner. In a footnote to "Women on the Breadlines," they commented:

> This presentation of the plight of the unemployed woman, able as it is, and informative, is defeatist in attitude, lacking in revolutionary spirit and direction which characterize the usual contribution to *New Masses*. We feel it is our duty to add, that there is a place for the unemployed woman, as well as man, in the ranks of the unemployed councils and in all branches of the organized revolutionary movement. Fight for your class, read The Working Woman, join the Communist Party.[11]

Despite her critics, however, Meridel struggled to develop a new form of literature — one which can be characterized as a "dialectical realism." Art, she believed, was of necessity social, and it was the function of the writer to be passionately committed to the expression of the political struggle.

> You wrote in the Socialist world more like a prophet, a conduit for the suffering of your people. A cry out... a whoop or a holler — more like the ballads of the people come to sing sorrow — a common sorrow. I also took this from the Hebraic prophets who were educators, singers, warners and opened the bundles of grief. I look upon writing as revealment, underground, subversive exposation (sic). I mean exposing the enemy. Remarks on Kansas caves, underground journals, newspapers, leaflets, posters, mass chants. To write to expose and to rouse, awaken, wake up. Watch out. Art as action, as deep image of struggle and not bourgeois reflection (L).

An important influence in the development of Meridel's aesthetic was the writings of Christopher Caudwell, a Marxist aesthetician. Caudwell called for a lyrical, evocative style because, he argued, it reflected collective inspiration: "nonrhythmic language is the language of private persuasion, and rhythmical language, the language of collective speech, is the language of public emotion."[12] This literature would portray characters self-conscious of themselves as social, political beings — a literature that would evoke the idea of relationship itself. Caudwell believed that it was only in the full realization of the interaction and dialectical encounter between outer reality (including political reality) and inner sense that true art comes to be known. It required a sensitivity to interaction and participation on the part of reader, writer and character.

> All art is conditioned by the concept of freedom which rules in the society that produces it; art is a mode of freedom, and a class society conceives freedom to be absolutely whatever relative freedom that class has attained to. In bourgeois art man is conscious of the necessity of outer reality, but not of his own, because he is unconscious of the society that makes him what he is. He is only a half-man. Communist poetry would be complete, because it will be man conscious of his own necessity as well as that of outer reality.[13]

Caudwell also insisted on a "concrete" awareness and expression of reality, believing that the artist has a duty to reflect the world as it "really" is: not abstractly, but personally through emphasizing the relationship inherent in the real world. The creation of art should reflect our social, collective experience:

> This concrete world of life which gathers up within itself as a rounded, developing whole the divorced and simpler abstract worlds of man and Nature, is the peculiar concern of the communist poet. He is interested in his own individuality, not in and for itself — a conception which conceals the contradiction that wrecked bourgeois society — but in its developing relation with other individualities in a communicating world that is not just a fluid amorphous sea, but has its own rigidity and reality. The communist poet is concerned to a degree never known before with the realization of all the values contained in the relations of human beings in real life.[14]

The goal of proletarian art was to bring the reader and writer together once again, in an encounter with the experience of human interrelationship in a social environment. But it was not just human interaction in itself that was to be experienced in this new aesthetic, but the sense of movement and process characterizing the basic rhythms of human life. The artist had a responsibility to depict not only the objective reality, but the process itself. Through engagement with the artist the observer is drawn into art, participates in art. "Indeed, it is largely this intimate relationship between reader and writer that gives revolutionary literature an activism and purposefulness long since unattainable by the writers of other classes."[15]

Caudwell also believed that art had a moral component, and that the artist was, of necessity, impelled to reflect not only class awareness, and the class struggle, but the moral goodness and rightness of that struggle. Art must be purposeful.

> The artist's task [is] to expound the profound meaning of events to his fellow-men, to make plain to them the process, the necessity, and the rules of social and historical development, to solve for them the riddle of the essential relationships between man and nature and man and society. His duty [is] to enhance the self-awareness and life-awareness of the people of his city, his class, and his nation ... to guide individual life back into collective life, the personal into the universal, to restore the lost unity of man.[16]

In this rich but neglected aesthetic tradition, Meridel's literary influence is only beginning to be understood. Art, according to Meridel, has as its primary responsibility the expression of the drama of human struggle and the illumination of the magic, pain, joys, and sorrows of human relationships. She advocated a new literature which emphasized the dynamic and participatory qualities of experience and was committed to evoking the collective aspirations of humanity. To Meridel, Marxism meant that art must *guide* consciousness in a new direction — not merely reflect the external reality. Instead, her commitment was to expressing the affective, passional, lyrical side of human experience. She also believed in the full significance of the dialectic. Change was not linear: revolutions could and did occur across a wide range of human experience. The role of the artist was to illuminate the social, collective significance of these struggles.

In evoking this particular collective sense, Meridel sought new literary patterns and rhythms which would most accurately reflect the process evoking participation and connection. Through passionate identity with the experience the reader and writer would be caught up in a new relationship. The rhythms of dance, song and movement are more indicative of her style, and reflect most clearly her commitment to evoking the sensuous quality of life and experience.

Meridel's writings are not flights *from* reality, but expressions of the linkages *between* the universal and the experiences common to all people. She goes directly to the experience and distills the literary reality from the universality of everyday lives. Rejecting the external, abstract symbolizing process, she turned instead to reflecting the inner, processual symbol-*making* experience. This resulted in art which celebrated the process of becoming, rather than leading the reader to a pre-ordained outcome. By engaging the reader in a process, a new symbol is created which draws together the myriad human expressions of struggle and becoming. Hers was an art committed to portray humanity as heroic; a humanity in the process of creating its own new future.

> But those that set us against each other dread the time when we find out that the myth and legend of our lives is the same in any language; that the tenderness and courage of our common struggle can be mutually known; when we find that the heroes known to us are the heroes known to others, warmed by the same blood in the cold, fed and nurtured on the same courage through dark nights in lonely posts, that it is man who rises laughing, gigantic, free in any language (SAB, 8).
>
> I wanted to write stories that could be read aloud, that people would laugh together over until they cried, embrace each other, slap each other on the back, lean forward looking to see if you got it all to the last drop, to explain, help you, as if the words were little lights striking, illuminating abysses of racial and national separation (SAB, 7).

History plays a very important role in Meridel's aesthetic, and it is a special sense of history as it reflects process. At first thought, this may seem to be in contradiction to her dynamic quality, her sense of immediacy and action. But realism expressed through the intensity of the moment does not base its reality in a linear, extensive passage of time. Each movement goes beyond the present through the illumination of an inner, intense, background or matrix of richness and depth. It is a very specific history which is reflected in her works: the history of the process of human liberation.

Meridel's insistence on grounding her art in the historical realities of the community, the people, and their struggles both politically and personally, resulted in a new aesthetic of relatedness. Literature could no longer be separate from the flux of experience. Incorporating the social base of history into literature grounded her aesthetic in the real, concrete world. A deep understanding of a people is a prerequisite to great art, she believes, and from the great wealth of language and actions of our pluralistic culture, she has struggled to create new images, legends, and myths.

A Dialogue on Literature and Art

N: This is going to be a difficult discussion for me, Meridel, mostly because I don't know a lot about literature and literary criticism and the like. Maybe a good place to begin is to quote what someone once told me. They said you were a Naturalist, both in terms of style and subject matter.

M: Well, I would disagree with that. I have always been very critical of the Naturalists. There are serious weaknesses of the Naturalist school, of American determinism defined in Dreiser, with its mechanistic psychology of ducts and glands, mechanical stimuli, the individual conceived as a mechanism driven by the equally mechanical drives of society.

Frank Norris, under the influence of Zola, wrote of a deterministic universe, both man and society expressing forces of huge power and chance, where wheat, oil, and the great combines almost take the place of nature, smashing out man and his conscious knowing, making him a helpless atom among other equally tangential atoms (SSM, 38).

N: Well it's true in some ways isn't it? They did show us the impact of huge forces controlling our lives. In a way, I see parallels between the Naturalists' portrayals of the great forces in our culture dominating us, and the Marxists' portrayal of the huge, capitalistic machine which we must struggle against.

M: Yes, But there is a great danger in the mechanistic qualities of their writing. This literature has dulled our sense as to what a human being is and his potential in our society. For example, Melville in *Moby Dick* has great passages presaging the sensuous unity of the new democratic man.

But the modern writers, Algren, Faulkner, Hemingway, and now Saul Bellow, Gold, Swados, the nihilists, the beatniks, the melancholy Danes, oppose the machine and monopoly, which they see dwarfs the individual and creates regimentation and impotence. Their work, gruelling and realistic, powerful and poetic as it is, does not serve the people in their need. Most often the result is a paralysis, an ambiguity that is disarming, a distortion of our democratic heritage, to the point of insanity; our history is made an illusion, the strength of our people appears bucolic, regional and illusory, past beliefs that would weave into the woof, appear to be only naivete and fanaticism (SSM, 38-39).

N:What is the alternative then? If you rejected the externalization of style of the Naturalists and their mechanical way of seeing reality, and the despair of the modern writers, what else was there? How about Gertrude Stein and that whole school they call the "Symbolists?" Was that a viable alternative to the mechanical perspective?

M: We might call them (since you're so fond of academic labels!) subjective idealists. This is marked by a removal in style and structure of the teller, which results in evasion. It amounts eventually to a psychic dislike of proximity. The so-called free individual is torn between objective capitalistic reality, and the subjective imaginative reality. This schism throws the individual further away from historical reality (TSS, n.p.).

Miss Stein explains this past-tense oblique prose, in which nothing happens, no scene or impact of the present takes place, by saying that in American life there is no present, that nothing actually takes place. What she means of course is that in decadent American bourgeois life nothing takes place, there is a muffling of event, a removal (JHB, 25).

The short story since Katherine Mansfield has been marked by a curious somnambulance of style, geographic removal in space and time, a romantic evasion and psychic equivocation which seems to suggest that life is cruel and bitter and memory is literature (TSS, n.p.).

N: You seem to be saying that both styles suggest alienation rather than connection. One extreme goes to the environment as mechanical, the other to hiding in the psychological self, the inner, secret world of the individual.

M: Yes, but of American proletarian life this is not true. American proletarian life is full of tremendous struggle, and the struggle must produce change as well. To express this, another technique is needed. In the world of the working class blows fall, hunger gnaws, walls are of cement, there is no remembrance of things past but a strong relish and embrace of the present for the conception of the future. Here there exists no equivocation of event. We do not need a muffled literature of dream and enchantment. The techniques of one class cannot do the work of another (JHB, 25).

N: That may be true, but I'm not sure or convinced that there cannot be the same intensity in a private experience. Sometimes my life is not all clear cut and sharp, sometimes things are equivocal and dream-like. I've really often found great strength in my personal experiences — sitting and thinking privately.

M: Of course your feelings are important! But there is a problem with carrying "privacy" to dangerous lengths. A lot of modern art is private, a lot of the poetry is just about the individual's suffering, it's very internal. In fact, I think all of bourgeois culture has been eccentric. It doesn't make any difference if anyone understands it or responds to it. It's esoteric. It's really an invitation to not enter reality, to not feel, but instead to abstract, like to abstract a painting. I like abstraction but not when it has nothing to do with anything. And Picasso said you never abstract an external object until you know all about it. You can draw it, feel it, even a chair. I mean you're all around it, the chair. It's a marvelous abstraction of sitting, of chairness. Well, I think that has something to do with the *praxis*. You need moving, if you're going to put the inner and outer together in an action which is going to change events — that's a movement. It's not static. In fact, that's the highest form of movement there is. Something like the yin and yang of the Eastern philosophy. You can't have anything without movement (T 13). There must be an objective and subjective collision in true art (Journals).

N: I'd like to explore some of the ideas you've just mentioned. You mentioned "class" analysis as needing different techniques. And proletarian art and literature and struggle. What do all of those political concepts have to do with art? Most people don't see any connection. In fact all the books about the Thirties say that art and politics are separate.

M: Well just your very statement shows that you can see them as separate. It's an academic question — this idea of the relationship of art and politics — or rather their lack of relationship, is what they want us to believe.

In American culture, in writing and in painting, and all aspects of art, there's too great a separation between the literary statement, the narration, and the action. We conceive of our artists as being the people who do not act, who do not become part of the struggle and the event and the history. Very early in my life I felt that people who wrote were also people who acted. Many of the IWW's and the old anarchists and socialists all had a tremendous feeling of the connection between what you thought, what you felt and what you did. Art must be the expression of the struggle and the communality of the people, not something dissociated or in some far abstract expression.

In my life, I've seen that whenever there's a struggle to free oppressed people, that the people become artists. There is no dissociation or dichotomy between art and action. You have to find the artistic expression from the *deed*, from the *action* (Film, outtakes).

N: Albert Hofstadter expressed it in this way: "but throughout the arts and in all the works, one essential universal prevails—the reciprocal ownness, the kinship of the subjective and objective components to one another, the inner truth to each other by which together, they form a true unity." And "In art man's spirit utters its meanings as unities of the subjective and objective which are not merely one-sided but reveal the essential bond between the two."[17] If the expression of the unity and co-experience of our lives is the goal of art, how do we move into this new consciousness of expression?

M: There is some kind of extremity and willingness to walk blind that comes in any creation of a new and unseen thing, some kind of final last step that has to be taken with full intellectual understanding and with the artist, a step beyond that too, a creation of a future "image," a future action... It is difficult because you are stepping into a dark chaotic passional world of another class, the proletariat, which is still perhaps unconscious of itself like a great body sleeping, stirring, strange and outside the calculated, expedient world of the bourgeoise. It is a hard road to leave your own class and you cannot leave it by pieces or parts; it is a birth and you have to born whole out of it. In a completely new body (FO, 22).

N: That reminds me of something Paula said when I interviewed her. She described your writings as being reflective of something she called "passional density" — similar to the concept of electron density. It's a feeling of intensity for things, for life. But where does the writer find this experience to be committed to?[18]

M: The poetry is in the bus station (T10).

N: People laugh when you say that.

M: Well before you can go to the people, you've got to believe. This is what has been so injured in our culture. You have to believe that all of culture comes from the oppressed. It's like Freire in *Pedagogy of the Oppressed* (New York: Seabury Press, 1968). The teachers think they're the source of knowledge, of culture and education. They believe that you should go to the people and somehow raise their consciousness. They cannot see that the oppressed are the only repository of culture in a monopoly capitalist system. All the morality and human- ism falls into the oppressed, because the oppressor can no longer even pretend to be human. He has to trash humanism — and so the only bearers of the culture of humanism are the oppressed. And if you don't believe that, forget it. You're not going to feel anything or see anything or record anything.

John: When I first read your stories in the old Anvil, *what really hit me was that it seemed to have the speech of other people in it, if you know what I mean. It was real language. William Carlos Williams talks about that, but he doesn't do that in his work.*

N: You've really captured the "people's" language and not the academicians words and forms and structures. A linguist friend of mine noted that you have recorded the Anglo-Saxon and Germanic base of our language rather than the Latin constructions. The rhythms, too, are non- Latin based, they're the rhythms of the everyday speech, the rhythms of an oral culture.

M: I think all the great language comes from the oppressed. They have nothing to defend. Why are the Indians great orators? Because they're not defending a lot of sludge (T10).

All lyricism, poetry, symbols, archetypes came from the working class. I learned speech from the farmers and workers. It was the only lyrical, poetic, living speech that I heard — on the street, the market, the farm, the church, the radical hall. And the farm women where I went and lived in order to see bodies that were alive and feel sympathy and communal love. I saw the middle class was without body, and without love and sensuality. I saw the farmers, workers, hoboes, socialists — people who gave their lives for a communal good (L).

N: Did a lot of writers agree with you? Political people? What about the Marxists? How did they feel about your writing?

M: It was hard to get even the Marxists to believe in the culture of the people. They have that elitist bureaucratic hierarchy thing — from the top. Now take a man like William Foster. When Browder was in power, Foster would come up to *The Worker* office every day, and he'd have a little essay, "What About the Worker?" And nobody would let him in! Every single day during that whole period he would appear. "The worker is suffering, what about the American worker?" he would say. There's a lot of stoic exceptionalism in Marxists — they're willing to organize the workers "for their own good," bring the gospel to them.

And people like Robert Minor. I was very much against what he did. He gave up his art to become an organizer. Now Mao wrote poetry. He took artists and writers and theater on the Great March. Even in our own history. Those covered wagons had musicians and singing and story telling. You can find newspapers in Minnesota in 1854 and on the front page is a poem by Whittier. Poetry was very important. People knew it.

Bill Haywood also loved people's poetry (T10). In the Middle West I think we try not to forget the IWW's. They spoke an American language, not English. Many of them were anarchists, many of them were only haters of the machine, but they started something. Like Johnny Appleseed who scattered the seeds for countless orchards in the Middle West, the IWW's brought countless thumbed copies of Marx (PL,137).

*Jim: Yes, even in the Twin Cities today. There's something
I never liked, that I think is a problem. The Left has this
attitude that art is not important.*

M: Yes, and they're turning into bureaucrats and
manipulators. How can we bring this back? I think it's a
true heritage. I'm in a minority, I'm su~e.

*N: In the Thirties there was this big movement to get back to
our "roots" of American culture. The Southern Agrarians
brought "regionalism" to our consciousness, didn't they?
They felt that we were moving too fast and that we were in
danger of losing our humanistic values. They were very
critical of industrial society. They said some marvelous
things — that we should have a relevant humanism
grounded in culture and traditions, not abstract ideals.
And that we should get back in touch with nature and
eschew industrialism and progress.*

M: But they really did a lot of damage to the health of the
arts in this country! In the Midwest, we broke with them.
The *Midwest* magazine grew out of the failure of the
Writers' Conference in Chicago in 1936. We revolted
against their "narrow regionalism" and their elitist
stance.

At that meeting, Phillips made a speech practically
saying that the people, the farmers, the workers were all
isolated and dumb because of capitalism. And of course
that they had no power and no culture. He said the
farmers couldn't love the land because it was capitalist
land. This really set me afire and I got up and said the
farmer *did* love the land, and we were here, and we loved
the land, and we were the basis of culture and he wasn't
— the intellectuals were the betrayers of culture. I ended
up crying! But that's what they were doing. Making this
bureaucratic, intellectual, inhuman, nonhuman kind of
thing of Marxism. And they were great and brilliant
with all their marvelous theoretic ideological speeches,
and none of us midwesterners — Jack Conroy, Nelson
Algren, Richard Wright — we were all just mavericks.

We didn't even know who, or have any ideological constructs — and I think Mike Gold then took up the sword against them — and Robert Minor (T10).

N: So they were really avoiding the political implications of regionalism?

Yes. In 1935, at that First Writers' Congress, I made a strong statement about regionalism. The spurious regionalism of the "little" magazine showed up the necessity of the artist to establish some roots not, however, in past history or reactionary regionalism; rather what we wanted was a regionalism of class roots, class history. [19] And in our preview of the *Midwest* magazine, we stated our criticism of these so-called Southern Agrarians.

This federation will be made up of the widest professional and cultural groups, united against fascist attacks, against war, and for the creation of a true historical and progressive regionalism which can be a carrier of the vital traditions of mid-American life, and serving as a unifying factor against the old regionalism which breeds reaction, which was retrogressive, seeking impossible reversions to the past, returns to the soil, and values tradition now as a self continuing and growing force but as a restrictive element only.

Such a regionalism divides a nation. What it values is the aristocratic tradition. Progressive regionalism would become a factor in national unity, it would build upon local traditions in which each region is rich, restoring them as national symbols — Haymarket, John Brown, the American dreams of freedom and creation which have moved against the money dreams of power. [20]

N: It sounds as if the Southern Agrarians were really committed to the kind of regionalism of escapism.

M: In the Midwest, we of the petty bourgeoisie and the working class, have been dissenters, individual madmen, anarchists against the machine; but now the Middle

Western mind is finding a place, sensing a new and vigorous interrelation with himself and others, which at last will give him the free association from the factual bourgeois and decaying reality to the true subjective image of the communal artist (PL, 138).

I think the Southern Agrarians were the most successful servants of the ambiguity — the sludge — shall we call them the Sludge School of Writing?! They did a yeoman's service to capitalist culture. Tate, Warren, Phillips.

John: Phillips from the old Partisan Review *— he said that we had to protect literature from the yahoos. We're the yahoos, I think.*

M: Tate — when he was here speaking to the librarians, made the statement that he was glad he came from a state where only five percent of the people could read. The yokel class didn't bother him. But those librarians did a great thing! You know, they do believe that people should read. When it came time to go down the receiving line and shake the Sacred Paw of the great writer, they all left! (T10).

N: You've spent a lot of time thinking and writing about the role of the writer — politically, aesthetically, culturally. I'd like to get a little more discussion going on things like style, theory, etc. Could you talk more about the process of writing?

M: Writing is primarily a sensuous and creative expression of life. Modern education for the most part is an apology for the distortion of a competitive, dog-eat-dog, system of life . . . They have set up a special image and called greed and competition "normal." Man automatically performs according to these images, and THIS IMAGE IS ANTAGONISTIC TO REALITY. Therefore, it is antagonistic to the creation of real art or real artists.

The chief qualities of sensibility and appreciation of

reality in flux are not deepened organically by the present education system. The opposite is true. They are destroyed completely and theory takes the place of organic knowledge... The writer must contact a reality in flux, without fixity, and he is inimical to the static form of an image. The university preserves with exquisite care the corpse of an old image whose spirit has long been dead. This image causes the neurosis of the education man. It is the worship of that WHICH STANDS FOR rather than that which IS. A system, a thing, a substitution for life. By the very nature of his craft, the creative writer must, above all, contact direct without intervening confusion — the very chaotic substances of life about him ... it is the writer's business to stand for the flux, to dynamically resist the habitual images and fetishes of his time and cut through the dying corpse with ruthless precision and create a NEW image, a new body of life (that will, I suppose, again accrue its barnacles of theory and have again to be murdered and reborn) (FEW, n.p.).

N: *Suppose we were to all shift to this new consciousness and new approach to writing. What kinds of things would be written? I know that being aware of class differences in our society is essential, and understanding the wisdom of oppressed people and their basic knowledge of life — but what else do we need to think about?*

Well you were asking about subjectivity before, and thinking it was important. There is a kind of subjectivity that we might talk about — a subjectivity that is not the spurious subjectivity of the bourgeois artists of personal defeat, subterfuge, and apology, but the subjectivity of the communal root image of a rising class (PL, 138).

When you are writing from inside of you, you're identifying with what you're writing and not just looking *at* your subject — not projecting them as an object. All narration is describing something. To describe something means you're outside looking at it and it's your opinion or your arrogance or your attitude that is being written down, more than it is any kind of interdependent relationship — love. Love is an identity with instead of an objective external thing. Everyone talks about love but you don't go in to find out what love is. Of being central to another person rather than outside of them. It isn't easy. When I write I sweat blood trying not to "tell." The more you narrate the more you externalize. Most writing is to externalize and objectify and actually kill what you're looking at (T15).

It's a patriarchal — let's not call it a male form — it's authoritative. The average story that moves to a crisis or a denouement or whatever you call it is a patriarchal movement, you're imposing on the reader. Murder stories or detective stories or the narration form of writing imposes on the reader a certain end. Stockhausen, the great composer of electronic music, says all the music of the nineteenth century moved toward the king. The structure of a symphony is a number of themes moving upward in a line towards a crisis. I can hardly listen to some of those symphonies ending with a bangboom. We don't need those kinds of structures (T5).

N: How do you avoid this killing or objectifying of something?

M: I don't know! This is a new field for scientists, for philosophers. If you're going to think in this way, it means a completely new attitude towards life. Completely new.

N: How has this new thinking changed your writing? I know in the past you've done your share of narrating, of telling — but I've also sensed a gradual development of that more circular, open style which focuses on sharing, drawing the reader into the experience.

M:Well one thing I did was do away with narration. Do away with telling about it. You have a feeling, don't you, in a lot of writing that it belittles the person? You don't have any heroes, this is the era of the "non-hero." It's all part of this concept of alienation. What is alienation but a high philosophical word for being an enemy? For being outside and being different. And objectifying, finally, until you're completely alone.

Most writing today is a superior person observing something that he's telling you about. Usually minimizing it. Saul Bellow, for example, can look at his character and reduce him to an absurd, absolute nothingness. At the same time, I suppose, making himself more important. Most of our writing is that way. Much of my writing in the past was me observing what was outside of me. I didn't have the sympathy for it (T15).

You need a relativity language instead of a pragmatic, analytic language... The main thing is you should write about the relationship and not the naming of it. Now Hemingway is naming it, and putting it down. He's telling you what to think about it, feel about it, what it is — he's confining it to his name of it.

N: But in this circular style of writing there's still the object there, the thing, isn't there?

M: No thing, no object.

N: I'm still not clear. Is what you're saying that there is really still an object, but now we learn to see it in its relationships?

M: No. You don't see it as a thing or as an object, you see. Its relationship *is* the reality, which is a process. If you make it an object, then you stabilize it. You should see it as a process.

Steve: It's a dialectical reality — even as you're there, it's changing.

M: You have to make these things part of your consciousness— it's going to change your writing, everything you do. It's your relationship passing another force and the interchange. Writing has to be about that interchange — what happens. Instead of alienating and analyzing and objectifying, it turns out that the writer and the reader and the thing that's written about, become one . . . Now Hemingway is manipulating the reader. He's imposing a hierarchy — *his* power, his vision upon you. It's sort of seduction.

We must get away from this dogmatic thing about the noun. It's the pragmatic convenience of seizure. I don't even think you should use description. I think it should be evoked by its relationship. Not described. When you describe you get again into a static place. But if you think about relationships you have to evoke them or recreate them in their relationship . . . There's too much description in poetry now! You know, I'm getting real tired of nature — somebody sitting on a rock looking at the elm. God, it's just them looking at the elm! Visenor said the other day, that naming like that is property. And it's like having the elm. It makes you feel good, because you've got it (T11).

But suppose you could write without being outside of what you were observing. This would be what we might call irrational, like, well, they call the quantum particle irrational. Nils Bohr who is also a very great poet, says that nothing happens to the minutest thing in the universe that doesn't affect everything. This central thing is so quick and so united and without boundaries or measurement or counting. There's no such thing as rationality except in relation to what we've set up. Time is something set up to reduce it so you can handle it, for example. So you can go to work every morning!

I think the artists — I think a lot of painters have done this more than the writers. And the musicians have done more, too (T15). The electronic musicians say that structure should be like the magnetic fields in relation to each other. Some people don't like electronic music because it's not going anywhere, not toward the crisis or the explosion or the denouement. But it has a structure of magnetic relationships. These musicians have done away with the linear progressive movement of music entirely. They talk about strong magnetic fields in juxtaposition to each other.

I think all science and all culture is more reflecting the feminine, or the thing that has been left out and trashed in Western culture is returning. There's a whole movement now, away from the authoritative, from the patriarchal. The narrative novel is patriarchal. Maybe it will disappear. I think it would be all right if it did! And I think women should look deeply into the patriarchal forms and understand those forms that are linear, invasive or manipulatory (T5).

N: How would adopting this circular consciousness affect how writing styles would change? I can see that you might look at things differently, express them differently, but how would style differ?

M: I think women have to really make their own language, use their own language. Language has been in the hands of the power structure. This language of women would probably be a subjective language, a language of lyricism, or a language of poetry — a language that will not be sterile. Analysis has become a way of seizing your mind. Now I'm not against analysis of power, but analysis is a way to trap you, to get you to think certain ways, to seduce you, or even rape you. Language has become a rape, a form of psychic rape. Like with all the "anti" communism, anti-this, anti-that — why you had to rape the whole nation in order to get them to submit to that — for a while anyway!

I also think women are afraid to use their language, I know I am! For a long time the woman language was excessive and hysterical. Somebody even told me the other day that I'm a "romantic." That's a put down because I've been called that by too many male editors.

I think language has another function beyond analysis. The other function is heat. Your language should heat you, you should rise up out of your chair and move . . . But this is deep subject. It's wracking me to pieces right now myself, to find out how I have been invaded and occupied by the enemy. How can you find what a woman's words are?

Listen to women talk. Women have a different rhythm and tempo. I think that's something we could catch. They talk differently. Listening to a good woman gossip in the country taught me more about women's words and language. And I think insane women reflect imagery and speech that is often female. Images are part of the whole thing, too, not only language. But what are the symbols? What are the images? What do you see as a woman?

A young woman told me after her baby was born, in that Spring when she looked at the landscape, she wept, because she realized that even the smallest kernel bursting open was in pain, that the whole world was opening. That's a marvelous conception, a marvelous statement. It's only the beginning of how you could write about the whole world giving birth, opening up. It's a very dangerous thing to do. You're entering into a new symbol, you're trying to get at a long-hidden symbol, that's been buried.

Look at rhythm, structure of music, or form — and what women painters are trying to do now. They structure something that isn't a cube or a square, something related to a woman's body. The round, the circular imagery (T5).

ENDNOTES

[1]Joseph Freeman, "Discussions and Proceedings," in Henry Hart, Ed., *First Writers Congress* (New York: International Publishers, Inc. 1935), p. 170.

[2] Malcolm Cowley, quoted in Daniel Aaron, *Writers on the Left* (New York: Avon, 1961), p. 353.

[3] Bill Haywood, quoted in Aaron, p. 34.

[4] William Phillips and Philip Rahv, "Recent Problems in Revolutionary Literature," in Louis Filler, Ed., *The Anxious Years: America in the Nineteen Thirties* (New York: G.P. Putnam's Sons, 1963), p. 341.

[5] Irving Howe, *Politics and the Novel* (New York: Avon, 1957), p. 22. Despite this rather rigid defense of "purity" in art and literature, it is particularly instructive to note that in the late Sixties research had unearthed the interesting historical tidbit that while Phillips and Rahv were intent upon keeping politics out of literature, their own literary journals, including the *Partisan Review*, were, in fact, being financially supported by the CIA from 1959 onward. These engineers of the anti-communist Left/liberal coalition, the culture-makers of pure art, were caught with egg on their political faces. See Christopher Lasch, *The Agony of the American Left* (New York: A. Knopf, 1969) and John Crawford, "Phillips' Political Odyssey Through Literature and Life," *The New York Smith*, 1, 3 (January 15, 1977), p. 42 passim.

[6] Aaron.

[7] Richard H. Pellis, *Radical Visions and American Dreams* (New York: Harper & Row, 1973), p. 186.

[8] Christopher Caudwell, *Illusion and Reality* (New York: International Publishers, 1947), p. 155.

[9] Irene Paull, letter to me, n.d.

[10] Harvey Swados, Ed., *The American Writer and the Great Depression* (New York: Bobbs-Merrill, 1966).

[11] Footnote to "Women on the Breadlines," *New Masses* (Jan. 1932), p. 7. Also in Swados.

[12] Caudwell, p. 26.

[13] Ibid., pp. 297-98.

[14] Ibid., p. 297.

[15] Phillips and Rahv, p. 339.

[16] Ernst Fischer, quoted in *Mayday Magazine*, 1, 1 (September 1974), p. 7.

[17] Albert Hofstadter, "On the Consciousness and Language of Art," *Philosophy East and West*, 19, 1 (January 1969), p. 13 and 4.

[18] Paula Zimmering, Interview.

[19] Meridel Le Sueur in Hart, p. 324.

[20] *Midwest Preview of Magazine to Come*, Meridel Le Sueur, Ed., p. 1.

"The World of Analysis is Dead"

Several years ago, in Albuquerque at the conclusion of a speech, Meridel was given a book that she "had waited for all my life." Her fascination with *The Tao of Physics*[1] which drew parallels between Eastern mysticism and modern Western physics lay not so much in the rather narrow focus of that study, but in the author's explanation of modern physics in readable, human terms.

In his book, Capra illuminates the cultural implications of this "new" science of physics, arguing for acceptance of the "bootstrap theory." This theory, or view of the world, em-

141

phasizes an ecological understanding of reality:

> The bootstrap theory constitutes the final rejection of the mechanistic world view of modern physics... In the new world view, the universe is seen as a dynamic web of interrelated events. None of the properties of any part of this web is fundamental; they all follow from the properties of the other parts, and the overall consistency of their mutual interrelations determines the structure of the entire web.[2]

This dynamic universe of interrelationship and balance parallels Meridel's own attitudes and perceptions of reality. This new, circular world view has profound implications for our culture, she believes, challenging as it does the cultural matrix of nineteenth century science and its themes of progress, linear time, and rational space. Le Sueur's rejection of these constructs initiated an exploration into new and different paradigms of cultural reality.

In a lecture in Minneapolis entitled "The Circle and the Square," Meridel outlined the meaning and significance of modern physics to her own circular philosophy:

> When Einstein in 1908 gave his first lecture on relativity, he asked scientists to forget everything they knew, to be as little children, to give up the concept of mechanical science of the nineteenth century, to understanding this new concept of relativity. Particle theory — it isn't hard to understand; if you really give away all those concepts that you have of counting from one to ten, of progress, of things acting in a logical, so-called common sense manner.
>
> Quantum theory and particle theory have nothing to do with common sense, or time. (The scientists) are looking at something that has no order of any kind in the sense that we know it. It has no consecutive linear life to it, has no loss of energy. It's a beautiful thing that happens — that while you're looking at it, it changes... it shows that no movement in the world can exist without changing every other movement. Humanism has always said this, but now it's a scientific fact that there is no outside. That there is only the interrelated movement on the inside. But you can't even say inside anymore. Nothing is removed or alienated (US).

This view challenges us to see the world in new ways: in terms of unpredictability, movement, interrelatedness. No longer is the observer to see the world as inner-outer, subjective-objective, or dualistic, but as a continuously present, simultaneously dynamic circular universe, a universe alive with vitality and excitement. There is no beginning-middle-end, no linear movement to *denouement*, but a constant celebration of the present, a celebration of "no loss of energy," a continuing renewing life force. Meridel describes her sense of this reality:

> What are the extensions of reality in my life? Extending in all directions alike, a faster turning sand painting with the entrance and egress in the middle and all plants, loves, children, time, struggles raying from it. Dante extended reality in these directions for his time. Van Gogh began to feel the wheel turn.
> I can never die. This part, this glowing can never die. This moment does not die. The fruit moment never dies. It is overlapped, lapped forward and backward. It does not hang alone outside the skin. It does not die. The LIVING moment never dies. Only the mechanical moment dies. In the mechanical is no seed, no weaving forward and backward.
> Evil is the only thing that dies. What is good hangs from some eternal tree and keeps on growing, dropping itself, folding over itself, bursting, growing into new youngness. It never dies. A living moment is for all time (Journals).

Meridel's allusions to time and the relationship of time to her circular philosophy are especially important in understanding the circular reality. She understands time in terms of a growth metaphor — similar in many ways to American Indian philosophies:

> In the cycle of root and bloom all appears in the calyx, newly risen, no intermittent silence or death, continuously present.
> Indians have no word for progress of time or sequence, for past, present and future. Their word for time means as near as we can conceive it, unfolding of bud and flower, the immediate germinal presence of the entire spiral of growth, instantaneous, reappearing.[3]

The full implications of this new concept of reality are yet to be comprehended. It is especially helpful therefore, to have thinkers like Le Sueur taking the new ideas and new thought and casting them in new, more familiar concepts. The world of the continuous present is a rich experience. And it is the all-encompassing symbol of the circle that Meridel has chosen to approximate this new, dynamic universe. All of reality is incorporated within a circular consciousness, and organic, holistic view of reality. At the center of this circular consciousness is a belief in the essential relatedness of all of reality. Inside the circle is a quixotic world — synthesis emerging out of dialectical tension. Ultimately it is a world of process and change, "ever not quite," the true contours of which we can only imagine.

> On the circle nothing is solid. All is movement. The reality is movement. To see the circular is to see the green sap, the jet upward, the wonderful magnetism toward ripening, the positive, the impulse, the great atomic impulse of gestation ripening living multiplying giving out (Journals).

There is action and excitement in the circular universe —an open infinite circle with neither beginning nor ending; moving spirally, into an "n-th" dimensional pattern.

> Relativity, simultaneity, things happening all at once, right and left, swiftness of the atom and energy, positions, all of these things have to be reflected.[4]
>
> The really great thing about modern physics is that there is no object. You cannot be an object looking at another object, because when you look at anything that is passing, you change it by looking at it, and it changes you by passing. There is no object. There is nothing external that you can measure, look at, reduce, minimize, conquer, have, take.
>
> That's what the circle really is. We talk about the circle. We really don't know what it is. It's nothing that you can have or that you can measure. It's immeasurable (T15).

This dynamic sense of the circle and of reality is what binds Meridel's universe together in intimate relationship. Circularity means that we are all *in* and *of* the circle — nothing is external to the reality. The reality *is* relationship — a concept which Einstein developed and which Heisenberg expanded upon in modern physics. One cannot choose to be related: one *is* related — to all life, to the land, to people,to the universe. Relationship, therefore, is no longer a mere "coming together" but a necessity of our very being. There is no Self, separated and discrete. The individual is known only in relation to others, and in fact, defines the self through the process of relationship. This sense of participation and belonging to the entire universe is the heart of Le Sueur's philosophy. From this circular sense of reality flows her ideas of art, politics, and the world in which we live. To live in this reality is to recreate the whole world, to give up our present understanding and move into a new consciousness, a new paradigm of explanation.

Sitting On A Hill In The Sun, We Talk

Meridel: One of the most dangerous concepts that we have in modern life is what I call the linear or male view of the world. It is aggressive, progressive. I saw this in my childhood in the midwest . . . the bright and terrible activity of progress, development, making money, grabbing everything in sight. It made a curious air of aggression, fear and even hate. We saw the frail villages, the wooden houses, prairies ravished, impermanent. A husk through which the immigrant poured, leaving nothing behind not even memory, going a lonely way all shouting to each other and unheard, alone and solitary. There was still the pioneer tension as if something was still to be done, something conquered, something overcome, and there is no longer anything to conquer and no longer an enemy . . . I went about the streets looking and looking, and what I saw seemed to be without pith or meaning, dark and spectral. And everyone peering through the strange air of a new continent perhaps saw the same thing, the outward busy, strenuous life and the pithless core, the black abyss . . . (CV).

Neala: I remember your story of Tradesman La Salle. He was like that — empty, alienated, and somehow driven into a future unknown. An air of compulsiveness. And profound loneliness somehow.

M: La Salle explored the upper reaches of the Ohio and the Illinois, probably alone, excited, secretive with his plans. He confided to no one. He had no friend, not even the wilderness. He was no adventurer, had no gusto for danger, but rather he was a timid man with the dreams of a king whose weapons were craft and endurance. He had a passion for his own exploits and the accomplishments of his own will. Secretly, moribund, he served his own will, speaking to no one, coiled tight, without confidant, man or woman. The wilderness was his woman, mother, companion: he could have no other because he could not have his will over another in that full way. He would have his sick, shy, frustrated will over the country, being too frightened to speak to a man or make love to a woman (TL, 37).

N: *In your story "Psyche" there was the same kind of person — a man unable to have a relationship with a woman. You describe his objectivity and alienation well: "With that unctuousness he collected, tramped, searched, dug, clipped, organized, recorded, spread knowledge, and left this woman beside him unexplored, bitterly bereft (PY, 26).*

M: Yes. It's even poor Mr. Ford and poor Mr. Nixon, those bodiless ghosts. They don't even have a body, let alone relationship. They can't put their arms out for another human being. The poor, deformed people. But it isn't just about men and women — it's architecture, painting, the way we go to war or don't go to war. I think it's important that we re-introduce the whole female cycle into the whole society, or we're going to die (T3).

N: *How do we move away from this sense of alienation? How do we change that lonely experience to one of intimacy, connection. And relationship?*

M: I think the only way to be whole is in the first place to understand that you do belong to society, you belong to women, you belong to children. I think wholeness is related to how much you are integrated in relationships. It all comes down to the relationship of everything. Otherwise you're going to have merely anxiety, dissection, disassociation, alienation — all of those popular things that psychiatrists are talking about (T13).

I belong to the new global age of plentitude! Where prose, poetry, everything must be about relatedness and expansion instead of contraction and alienation. Young people now have this. They really can expand and include, rather than exclude. We are moving into becoming related *to*, rather than alienated *from*. All dynamics comes from relationship, dialectics of change.

Women can really express this because they're on the round, not on the linear. Getting into the global world means there's no longer the linear world — no time, no progress. You can only progress along a straight line. Our ecological problems are a result of being on a straight line. We imagine we'll never return, because a straight line doesn't return. You think you can crap anywhere and do anything you want. But if you're on a circle, what you do *here* returns *here*, and the shit falls on you. If you think circularly, you could never pollute the earth, because you would know that it would return something that is foul.

I call this the feminine consciousness. The world has gotten into trouble because of the "male" philosophy. By that I don't mean just men, but men do represent it. The female, the mothering element of the earth — men have got to become mothers and nourishers instead of exploiters and seizers (T3).

N: I think we're still committed to those ideas of progress and objectivity. But I think more and more people are beginning to question whether you can reduce everything to statistics and facts. Our new awareness of energy, too, has made thinking circular a possibility. But what we're really talking about is changing the whole culture!

M: (She nods in agreement.) Those ideologies do nothing but strangle you and diminish the possibility for growth. And this is where the action of the writer or creative worker of any kind comes in. It is an action of belief, of full belief. There is some kind of extremity and willingness to walk blind that comes in any creation of a new and unseen thing, some kind of final last step that has to be taken with full intellectual understanding and with the artist, a step beyond that too, a creation of a future "image" a future action that exists in the present even vaguely or only whispered, or only in a raised arm, or a word dropped in the dark but from these, because of full belief, he will produce a movement, even a miraculous form that has not hitherto existed . . . It is difficult because you are stepping into a dark chaotic passional world . . . you cannot leave the old world by pieces or parts, it is a birth and you have to be born whole out of it. The creative artist will create no new forms of art or literature for that new hour out of that darkness unless he is willing to go all the way, with full belief, into that darkness (FO, 23).

N: But it's really hard to be this passional person when everybody around you is operating on a different frequency! Any expression of excess, of feeling, of passion (except in bed) is frowned upon in our culture. I end up not saying anything, finally, and retreating into myself.

M: That's the other extreme, almost as dangerous. There you are not connected with anything. I think you become dissociated when you are alone, when you don't have a sense of this being together. The natural woman knows this. She's together because she is linked to this knowledge in her body of being related to something besides her own ego or somebody's vision of her. If you don't belong to a body, or are part of some cosmic body, then you're nothing (T13).

N: The body. In our society today, it has a clinical connotation. The only time we talk about bodies with one another is when we discuss medical things. And touching! We are all so afraid to touch or be close to each other — especially between the sexes. Psychically and physically we deny the reality of the body.

M: Yes, many people are this way, alienated from each other, alienated from their own bodies. Perhaps they need more than anything some colossal group belly to give them birth . . . These people are unconnected and building up mental bulwarks. Never approaching the deep self, they cut off the channels to refreshment and recreation. Maybe they needed some birth more than their mother gave them — and it would have to be a physical birth. They could have no mental births.

N: You mean non-intellectual?

M: Yes. Nothing they could *think* would make any difference at all — nothing they could *know*. A man who knows so much, who makes questionnaires and yet doesn't know the flesh of his wife cannot question her at all about what is in her. Unless a man can take a woman, apprehend her in this tender, living way, he kills her. It would be better not to have anything to do with sex until one can feel and bloom and flare out physically and tenderly towards another (Journals).

We can't have dead people. They have to be struck to fire in the bodies of others, in struggle. This is the only fire that is left alive, under the ash. This passionate identity must be felt by all . . . and made by all. Not intellectually or merely commitment to a "cause," jumping from one cause to another, but in the body, in the passions, in the deepest identity, the true relationship. This is the true image rising out of the carnage (T13).

N: Relationship then, is both this private and collective experience at the same time? Are you saying that this sense of human solidarity is necessary to our understanding of the world? And ourselves?

M: Identifying with the people . . . I only partly know what I am seeing, feeling, but I feel it is the real body and gesture of a future vitality . . . I am one of them, yet I don't feel myself at all. It is curious, I feel most alive and yet for the first time in my life I do not feel myself as separate. I realized then that all my previous feelings have been based on feeling myself separate and distinct from others, and now I sense sharply faces, bodies, closeness (IWM, 187). With one touch, one feel, you can construct the whole world — the real world. But without that, you have no ground to stand on (Journals).

A good example of this is our work on the film. This is what communality is. It is heat and ripeness and growth. This is what creation is, creation of everything, anything. Your love of my work, my love of yours. What you did was

make a meadow for my words and produced an entirely
different mutation. A new visible image. I am like a
tumbleweed tearing over the prairie dropping seed in
sterile deserts. Being parched, flooded, ignored and
trashed — and to find this meadowed loam, this great
woman loam — together we have made a new crop! (L).
We're all like pears, really. I remember reading
somewhere that pears, when they're ripening, emit some
sort of gas, and that you have to have the pears together
for them to ripen. They won't ripen by themselves,
isolated from other pears (T3).

*N: Relationship. It seems to have room in your philosophy
for both the individual and the group, for both the subjective
and objective.*

M: Yes. And women know this. Women represent subjective life that has been thrown out by the male objective
world. The objective world is male. And the subjective
world, which is the inner psychic world, or whatever you
want to call it, has been trashed. To express that
subjective world is insane. This I think is one of the
injuries of how our world has split the objective and
subjective. You have schizophrenia. That's what we've
done. In a healthy person the objective and subjective
have to be together. I mean they must alternately flow,
praxis, they call it now. It means the action upon the
world from the objective and subjective together — but
moving to action, not remaining inaction (T13).

I think that analysis, the world of analysis is dead.
Even science has abandoned it, the world of cause and
effect. They're talking about simultaneity, the return of
everything. They're looking at something that has no
linear movement. It's a globular atomic movement (T3).

Changing the world. If you're going to change the
world you can't just do it from either one — the subjective
or objective. You have to have a *praxis* between them
which moves into action, which changes the nature of
things. I think this is the meaning of revolution (T13). I

am not satisfied until I am able to be a whole, sensuous being with all the underlying forces being born directly from the womb of feeling without intercession of the mind, so that things will BE, exist — so that there is the real world and not the ghostly world (Journals).

ENDNOTES

[1] Fritjof Capra, *The Tao of Physics* (Berkeley, CA: Chambala, 1974).

[2] Ibid. p. 286.

[3] Le Sueur, "Preface," *Corn Village* (Sauke City, WI: Stanton & Lee, 1970), p. 11.

[4] Kirkpatrick, p. 9.

[5] Film Outtakes.

"America: Song We Sang Without Knowing"

A lion does not write a book. The broken trail of the people must be followed by signs of myriad folk experiences in story, myth, legend, reflecting the struggle to survive; in the spore of old newspaper, folkway marking the rituals of birth, death, harvest, planting, in the embroidery on the pillow, the democracy quilt. These signs are not to be found easily or read lightly, measured like rock, estimated as metal. Folkways are malleable. They disappear as inland rivers do and reappear to flood a continent. . . Folklore is the hieroglyphics of all man's communication, both obvious and subterranean, as he struggles with growing society, changing tools, to create a place, a community, a nation (North Star Country, 4).

Meridel began her journey through America, with an eye to penetrating those cultural patterns and images which explain what it means to be an "American." Seeking the source and root of our collective experience, searching the hearts of people and relationships, the forces and energies of radical movements and power structures, she has illuminated the magic of a whole people, embracing them in the great circle of her vision.

Hers was no high-blown analysis, no objective dissection of a culture, no statistical study. Instead, she sang a great poetic song, synthesizing our joys, our sorrows, our continuity and complexity. The tensions and seemingly irreconcilable contradictions inherent in every human personality and culture are faithfully and lovingly recorded in her works. But beyond her songs, beyond her poems, beyond her stories, lies her great love for her people. And as we understand her love for the American people and the land, we come to see ourselves and our culture in a new light. Hearing her love song we learn to sing our own. In her words we hear our own words transformed into a new dimension; mingled with the fragrances of the rich diversity of our culture, our song is deeper, more intense, more collective.

A Culture of Love

Meridel sees America as many cultures. In articulating the song we sang without knowing, she refused to be intimidated by the immensity of the task of this multiple song. Our new song, our new vision of American culture includes not only our European, white heritage, but the roots of all Americans — Blacks, Indians, Chicanos, workers, women, children. The idea of a collective autobiography is an apt description of how she achieves her integration. At times intensely personal and revealing, at others intensely collective, the movement and flow of a rich and diverse people are transformed into a vision of a whole people, of humanity.

Seeing our experience pluralistically is only the first step, however. The understanding of culture in terms of its dialectics brings alive the energy which drives the culture, brings it to life. The random movements of people and causes are sharpened as they come to spark one another in their relationships. Cultures exist and develop and change as part of an on-going process. They move dialectically. The conflict, the struggle, is an essential quality of human culture, according to Meridel, and the epic qualities of humanity's growth are sharpened in the *praxis*.

It is fashionable to say we have no culture in America. This is the louse commenting on the lion. The creative roar of democratic intercourse has sounded in our country since the starving and robbed Indians organized the first farmers' revolt... It spoke through the Grange, the Farmers Alliance and Populist party. The frontier organizations cradled a new man who boldly sought to grasp control of government by the ballot, created his own newspapers, printed books of poetry, wrote songs sung in prairie picnics, spoke in long periods of oratory, held together a cultural dream of cooperation and coalitions of the future. As long as there is work on wood, or metal, or upon the soil, or as man bears down and changes the nature of his work, and his social relationship, there will be a culture of work and struggle. Community of suffering, of need, of menace makes the democratic meeting out of which comes struggle, organization, the poem, the song (PS,).

The dialectical tensions that Meridel sees in the American culture interact simultaneously at many levels. Collectivity counterpoints individualism; the radicals challenge the establishment; the aesthetics of collective passion are balanced against the individualistic narrative; the linear, rational world is in praxis to the organic, circular world. All these tensions provide the *praxis*, the action in the American culture.

While these contradictions and tensions can co-exist, there are, ultimately, choices to be made. Every choice, every action, is laden with significance and must be evaluated in light of values inherent in a radical interpretation of history. Only when weighed in relation to human values, do ideas and movements take on cultural significance for Meridel. The purposive struggle to overcome repression and exploitation is the fulcrum on which Meridel rests her evaluation of contradictions within the culture. The song we sang without knowing is a particular song, with a particular direction and purpose. It is a song which reflects the struggle to be free to build a collective society.

Ultimately, however, Meridel's sense of America is an aesthetic one — lending our experience its depth and intensity, its expression and vitality. The task of explaining culture may confound historian and philosopher alike and fall instead within the province of the poet. Who but the poet can integrate the myriad expressions of the American? Who but the poet can integrate Puritanism and the modern day covens? the abolitionist and the Ku Klux Klan? the anarchist and the capitalist? the right to life and the rape of the land? the Pentagon budget and the welfare mother? the commune and the computer? or hand-milled wheat and McDonalds hamburgers?

Who but the poet?

The creation of poetic imagery provides an important means of experiencing the integration of the action and the rich diversity of our culture. Find the symbols — illuminate the culture. Integrating the rhythms and energies of a culture creates vital symbols and metaphors — symbols which portray the people in their movement, their dance. The artist must be, first of all, committed. Committed to involvement and engagement with the dialectical process of cultures at their most intimate level. Art must not merely reflect, but inspire. It is only through participation that the evocative power of symbols and images emerges. The Spanish poet Garcia Lorca once wrote: "The poem, the song, the picture is only water taken from the well of the people. It should be given back to them in a cup of beauty so that they may drink, and in drinking, understand themselves."

The Song We Sing

One of the delights of reading Meridel's journals was the discovery of little "stories" — short word pictures which seemed to distill great truths in their simplicity. One of my favorites reflects the essence of the "song we sang without knowing" — the incredible optimism and enduring persistence of the human spirit that Meridel has captured in her works, and which has served to inspire and sustain her own optimism and idealism. In the dialogue we hear her great faith in the power of the people:

> Here is the story of Carson Berfield and his encounter with the Indian.
> His irrascibility and his feeling that his power had leaded (sic) away
> from him.
> He said: "I wish I could feel sure as you do."
> The chief said: "Your people have power."

And Meridel responds to her own created dialogue:

> It is this power that is coming to me. I will know. All I have to do is wait
> for it to come and get stronger. It will be a quiet power. It will have
> songs (Journals).

We can almost hear her singing in a big voice the great song of the American people, reflecting their great power and her great love for them, for the land, for the "circle of immensity" that is our collective experience. It is a song of struggle, a song of pain, and ultimately a song of joy and celebration. It is a song to which we all know the tune as we tap our feet to the rhythms of working, building a new society, a new world. From the democratic village in our past, the neighborhoods and towns of our present, to the global village in our future, the song America sang without knowing we now sing with a big voice. As we join Meridel's voice, and move through the present to the future, she gives us some hints of our future song:

> Global consciousness, a global world, a new world. Not of global
> imperialism, but human collectivism; not cultural imperialism but
> global consciousness of new human relationships; not isolation and fear,
> but global solidarity; not the antithesis, but the synthesis; not the power
> that disintegrates, kills; but power of the people. A power that relates to
> energy to everything, generates and does not consume. The ego, the I,
> will turn into the global we (US).

A Song for Tomorrow

> The people are a story that never ends, a river that winds and falls and
> gleams erect in many dawns; lost in deep gulleys, it turns to dust, rushes
> in the spring freshet, emerges to the sea. The people are a story that is a
> long incessant coming alive from the earth in better wheat, Percherons,
> babies, and engines, persistent and inevitable. The people always know
> that some of the grain will be good, some of the crop will be saved, some
> will return and bear the strength of the kernel, that from the bloodiest
> year some survive to outfox the frost (NSC, 321).

A song of survival, a song of struggle. The story of a woman and of a culture — this is Meridel's song, and the song we sang without knowing. She was born two generations after the Civil War into the Progressive Era and the rise of American feminism. Through two World Wars, the Great Depression, and the coming of the Age of Nuclear Power, she dedicated her life to documenting the pain and joy of twentieth century America. Her passion was always for the prairie and the wind-swept faces of the people. In the great middle space of the continent her unhampered vision found home.

> My prairie people are my home
> Bird I return flying to their breasts.
> Waving out of all exiled space
> they offer me refuge
> To die and be resurrected in their
> seasonal flowering.
> My food their breasts
> milked by wind
> Into my starving city mouth (RAR, 23).

Key to Le Sueur Quotes in Text

A......... *Annunciation.* Los Angeles: Platen Press, 1935.

APNC.... "The Ancient People and the Newly Come." *Growing up in Minnesota.* Chester G. Anderson, Ed. Minneapolis: University of Minnesota Press, 1976, pp. 17-46. (autobiographical).

C......... *Crusaders.* New York: The Blue Heron Press, Inc., 1955.

CV....... *Corn Village.* Sauk City, Wisconsin: Stanton & Lee, 1970.

DT....... "The Dark of the Time." *Mainstream,* 9, 7, August 1956, pp. 12-21.

DR....... "How Drought Relief Works." *New Masses,* XX, 8, August 18, 1936, pp. 14-16.

FEW..... "Formal 'Education' In Writing." no citation, n.d.

FO....... "The Fetish of Being Outside." *New Masses,* February 1935, pp. 22-23.

G......... *The Girl.* New York: West End Press, 1978.

H........ *The Horse. Story,* 15, 1939, pp. 66-104.

JE....... "Journal Excerpts." *The Lamp in the Spine,* Summer-Fall 1974, pp. 94-126.

JHB...... "Join Hand and Brain." (Book review) *World To Win* by Jack Conroy. *New Masses,* XVI, 2, July 9, 1934, p. 25.

MWU.... "Milk Went Up Two Cents," *Black and White,* 2, 3, 1940, pp. 26-29.

NSC...... *North Star Country.* New York: Duell Sloan & Pearce, 1945.

OC....... "Excerpts from "The Origins of Corn." *New American: A Review,* 2, 3, Summer-Fall 1976, pp. 20-23.

PL....... "Proletarian Literature and the Middle West." *American Writers' Congress.* Henry Hart, Ed. New York: International Publishers, 1935, pp. 135-138.

PS....... "People are the Story." *The People Together.* Minneapolis: People's Centennial Book Committee of Minnesota, 1958, pp. 1-2.

PY....... "Psyche." *Windsor Quarterly,* III, 1, Fall 1935, pp. 17-27.

RAR..... *Rites of Ancient Ripening.* Minneapolis: Vanilla Press, Inc., 1975, 1976.

SAB...... "Shalom Aleichem Belongs to the People." *Jewish Life,* VI, 5, March 1947, pp. 7-8.

SL .... "Sequel to Love." *Anvil*, January 1935, pp. 106-108.

SSM...... "Saga of the Steel Mills." (Book review) *The Magic Fern* by Phillip Bonosky. *Mainstream*, 14, 10, October 1961, pp. 37-44.

TFG...... "They Follow Us Girls." *Anvil*, January 1935, pp. 106-108.

TG .... "The Girl." *Yale Review*, 26, December 1936, pp. 369-381.

TH .... "The Hell With You, Mr. Blue!" *Fantasy*, 7, 1, 1941, pp. 11-18.

TLS ...... *Tradesman La Salle*. *Manuscript*, 3, October 1936, pp. 33-57.

TSS ...... "The Short Story." *Manuscript News*, 2, October 1935, no pp.

CS .... "The Circle and the Square." Speech presented to Minneapolis Unitarian Society, October 24, 1976. Tape.

WB....... "Women on the Bread Lines," *New Masses*, January, 1932, pp. 5-7.

WR....... "The Wheat Ring." Edited and adapted by Mary Williams. *North Country Anvil*, 13, October-November 1974, pp. 43-47.

WRF ..... "Where the Rain Falls: A Reverie—the Next Hundred Years." *The People Together*. Minneapolis: People's Centennial Book Committee of Minnesota, 1958, pp. 47.

Tapes & Interviews

T1 — Baker, Mike. Interview, 1974. 1 hr.

T2 — Le Sueur, Deborah. Interview, not recorded, August 1976.

T3 — Le Sueur, Meridel. Interview, October 25, 1974, 1 hr.

T4 — Le Sueur, Meridel. Interview on "Land," June 11 and 15, 1977, 3 hrs.

T5 — Le Sueur, Meridel. Women's History Lectures and Discussions, Chrysalis Women's Center, 1974, 8 hrs.

T6 — Le Sueur, Meridel. Poetry Reading, Neuman Center, May 22, 1976, 1 hr.

T7 — Le Sueur, Meridel. Poetry Reading and Discussion, Marxist Club, University of Minnesota, March 2, 1977, 1 hr.

T8 — Le Sueur, Meridel, Bill Maxine and Mary Maxine. Conversations, July 27, 1976, 2 hrs.

T9 — Le Sueur, Meridel, Rachel Tilsen and Neala Schleuning. Conversations, September 1976, 3 hrs.

T10 — Le Sueur, Meridel, John Crawford, Jim Dochniak and Neala Schleuning. Conversations, October 11, 1976, 3 hrs.

T11 — Le Sueur, Meridel and others. Meetings on *North Star Country*, from May 29, 1977, June 1, June 12. 6-8 hrs.

T12 — Marvy, Darlene. Interview, September 1976. 30 min.

T13 — Twin Cities Women's Film Collective. Meeting. Meridel and others, 1975, 4 hrs.

T14 — Twin Cities Women's Film Collective. Meeting. Meridel and others, September 25, 1975, 2 hrs.

T15 — Twin Cities Women's Film Collective. Meeting. Meridel and others, March 1976, 2 hrs.

T16 — Twin Cities Women's Film Collective. Outtakes from "Continuous Woman," 1973, 30 min.

T17 — Zimmering, Paula. Interview June 29, 1976, 1 hr.

Selected Bibliography of
Meridel Le Sueur

Books

Annunciation, Los Angeles: Platen Press, 1935.

Crusaders. New York: Blue Heron Press, Inc., 1955.

The Girl. New York: West End Press, 1978.

North Star Country. New York: Duell, Sloan & Pearce, 1945.

Rites of Ancient Ripening. [Poems]. Minneapolis: Vanilla Press, Inc., 1975.

Worker Writers. Handbook, Minnesota Works Progress Administration, n.d. [1939]. Reprinted West End Press, 1982.

Zapata. Unpublished novel.

Children's Books

Chanticleer of Wilderness Road: A Story of Davy Crockett. New York: Alfred A. Knopf, 1951.

Conquistadors. New York: F. Watts, 1973.

Little Brother of the Wilderness: The Story of Johnny Appleseed. New York: Alfred A. Knopf, 1947.

The Mound Builders. New York: F. Watts, 1974.

Nancy Hanks of Wilderness Road. New York: Alfred A. Knopf, 1949.

The River Road: A story of Abraham Lincoln. New York: Alfred A. Knopf, 1954.

Sparrow Hawk. New York: Alfred A. Knopf, 1950.

Novellas

The Bird. New Caravan, ed. A. Kreymborg et al. New York: W. W. Norton, 1936, pp. 177-223.

The Horse. Story, 15, 1939, pp. 66-104.

O Prairie Girl Be Lonely. Cross Section, 1947, ed. Edwin Seavers. New York: Simon & Schuster, 1947, pp. 40-71. Now included in *The Girl.*

Tradesman La Salle. Manuscript, 3, October 1936, pp. 33-57.

Collected Short Stories

Corn Village. Sauk City, Wisconsin: Stanton & Lee, 1970. Includes: "Corn Village," "Persephone," "Gone Home," "Annunciation," and "Rites of Ancient Ripening."

Harvest. New York: West End Press, 1977. Includes: "What Happens in a Strike," "Women on the Breadlines," "Harvest," "Fudge," "Autumnal Village," "God Made Little Apples," "To Hell with You, Mr. Blue," and "We'll Make Your Bed."

Salute to Spring. New York: International Publishers, 1940. Reprinted 1977, 1981. Includes: "Corn Village," "No Wine in His Cart," "Fable of a Man and Pigeons," "A Hungry Intellectual," "The Girl," "Annunciation," "Biography of My Daughter," "The Dead in Steel," "Tonight Is Part of the Struggle," "Farewell My Wife and Child and All My Friends," "Salute to Spring," and "I Was Marching."

Song For My Time. New York: West End Press, 1977. Includes: "Song For My Time," "Eroded Woman," "Summer Idyl," "American Bus," "Of This Time, Upon This Earth," "The Dark of the Time," and "The Return of Lazarus."

Women on the Breadlines. New York: West End Press, 1977. Includes: "Women on the Breadlines," "Sequel to Love," "They Follow Us Girls," and "Salvation Home."

Ripening. New York: Feminist Press, 1982, Elaine Hedges, ed. Includes: Selections from *Crusaders, North Star Country,* "The Ancient People and the Newly Come," "Persephone," "Spring Story," "Wind," "The Laundress," "Our Fathers," "Annunciation," "Women on the Breadlines," "Women are Hungry," "I Was Marching," "Cows and Horses are Hungry," "Women Know a Lot of Things," "O Prairie Girl Be Lonely," "The Girl," "Gone Home," "Eroded Women," "The Dark of the Time," "A Legend of Wilderness Road," "The Origins of Corn" excerpt, "Rites of Ancient Ripening," "I Light Your Streets," "Doan Ket," Journal excerpt, *Memorial* excerpt.

Uncollected Short Stories

"Afternoon." *Dial,* 84, May 1928, pp. 386-98.

"Alone in Chicago," *Anvil,* 5, March-April 1934, pp. 5-7.

"American Bus." *Masses & Mainstream,* 8, 12, December 1955, pp. 26-36.

"The American Way." *Midwest,* November 1936, p. 5 and passim.

"Beer Town." *Life in These United States.* New York: Scribners & Sons, 1933, pp. 156-59.

"Blues in B Flat." *Mademoiselle,* November 1946, p. 200 passim.

"Breathe upon These Slain." *Kenyon Review,* 7, Summer 1945, pp.

399-418. Also in *O. Henry Memorial Award Prize Stories of 1946*, ed. Herschel Brickell. Garden City, N.Y.: Doubleday & Co., Inc., 1946.

"Christmas and the Child." *Parents*, December 1934, p. 16 passim.

"The Derned Crick's Rose," *Mainstream*, 9, 7, August 1945, pp. 12-21.

"Dust," *The American Year: Nature Across America*, ed. Henry Hill Collins, Jr. New York: G. P. Putnam's Sons, n.d., pp. 71-73.

"Evening in a Lumber Town." *New Masses*, 1, 3, July 1926, pp. 22-23.

"Father of the Earth." *The Fountain*, March 1942.

"The Glory of Robert Emmet." *Masses & Mainstream*, 5, 4, April 1952, pp. 38-47.

"Holiday." *Pagany*, 1, Spring 1930, pp. 87-99.

"Home Sweet Home." *Decade*, IV, 3, First Quarter 1943, pp. 21-26.

"Home Was a Million Streets." *New Masses*, April 8, 1941, p. 18.

"Inheritance." Looking Forward: Sections of Works in Progress by Authors of International Publishers on the Occasion of Its Thirtieth Anniversary. New York: International Publishers, 1954, pp. 33-41.

"Iron Country." *Masses & Mainstream*, 2, 3, March 1949, pp. 53-60.

"Milk Went Up Two Cents." *Black and White*, 2, 3, 1940. pp. 26-29.

"The Miracle." *Pagany*, III, 2, April-June 1932, pp. 1-16.

"Morning." *Literary America*, VI, 4, August 1934, p. 17 passim.

"My Town." *New Republic*, 84, September 25, 1935, pp. 175-78.

"A Night in the Woods." *Masses & Mainstream*, 8, 12, December 1955, pp. 26-36.

"The Orchard." *Manuscript*, 1, 6, December 1934, pp. 70-75.

"People in the Heat." *Dubuque Dial*, 2, 1934, pp. 70-75.

"Poets of Wood and Word." *Common Ground*, 5, 2, Winter 1945, pp. 36-40.

"Psyche." *Windsor Quarterly*, III, 1, Fall 1935, pp. 17-27.

"The Root." *California Quarterly*, 4, 1, 1954, pp. 32-37.

"Slow Train." *New Masses*, December 8, 1942, pp. 12, 14.

"Spring." *Woman's Home Companion*, April 1934, pp. 62-63.

"Spring Came On Forever." *Plain Song*, 1, Spring 1967, pp. 5-17.

"The Story of Dan Garrison." *New Masses*, January 6, 1942, pp. 12-13.

"Sunday." *Decade*, 11, 6, March-April 1942, pp. 1-9.

"Sure, Honey." *New Anvil*, June-July 1939, pp. 5-8.

"Sweet Beulah Land." *Collier's*, October 5, 1946.

"The Trap." *Scribner's*, 93, January 1933, pp. 27-32.

"The Way It Seems." *Dubuque Dial*, 1, 1934, pp. 22-24.

"This Is From David." *Story*, 17, 1940, pp. 91-101.

"Tiger! Tiger!" *Harper's Bazaar*, March 15, 1939, pp. 115-17.
"Wild Buffalo." Unpublished.

Selected Articles

"Benson of Minnesota." *New Masses*, September 6, 1938, pp. 8-10.
"Citizen Dove's Letter," *Sunday Worker*, March 15, 1942, p. 6.
"The Dakotas Look Back on a Trail of Broken Treaties." *Worker*,
   March 19, 1950, p. 4.
"The Farmers Face a Crisis." *New Masses*, 1936, pp. 9-10.
"The Fetish of Being Outside." *New Masses*, February 1935, pp.
   22-23.
"The First Farmer's Revolt: A Tale of the American Indian's Fight
   for His land." *Mainstream*, 15, 3, March 1962, pp. 21-26.
"Formal 'Education' In Writing," no citation, n.d.
"How Drought Relief Works." *New Masses*, 20, 8, August 18, 1936,
   pp. 14-16.
"The Land of the Free Seen From a Bus." *The American Spectator*,
   December 1935, pp. 6-7.
"Lumbering in Minnesota." *The Worker*, April 20, 1945, sec. 2, p. 2.
"Midwest Writers Conference." *Pacific Weekly*, 5, November 16,
   1936, p. 324.
"Minneapolis Counts Its Victims." *New Masses*, October 1, 1935, pp.
   12-15.
"Murder in Minneapolis." *New Masses*, 12, 6, August 7, 1934, pp.
   12-13.
"Of These We Sing." *Daily Worker*, August 30, 1940, p. 7.
"The People Demand." *New Masses*, 17, 1935, pp. 14-15.
"Proletarian Literature and the Middle West." *American Writers
   Congress*, ed. Henry Hart. New York: International Publishers,
   1935, pp. 135-38.
"Send Off." *The Worker*, April 9, 1944, p. 4.
"She Heard the Great Voice of Mother Bloor." *The Worker*, August
   30, 1942, p. 6.
"Sholom Aleichem Belongs to the People." *Jewish Life*, VI, 5, March
   1947, pp. 7-8.
"The Short Story." *Manuscript News*, 2, October 1935, n.p.
"The Sleepwalkers." *New Republic*, 75, August 2, 1933, pp. 313-14.
"Under A Swinging Light in a Schoolhouse." *The Worker*, November
   21, 1954, p. 3.
"Wartime County Fair." *New Masses*, January 18, 1944, pp. 13-15.
"The Wheat Ring." Edited and adapted by Mary Williams. *North*

Country Anvil, 13, October-November 1974, pp. 43-47.

Poetry

"Corridos of Love." *Mainstream*, 15, 6, June 1962, pp. 23-25.

"Demeter's Weeping Stone." *Moons and Lion Tailes*, II, 1, 1976, pp. 32-34.

"From the Furrow." *Masses and Mainstream*, 4, 3, March 1951, pp. 35-38.

"Gateway." *Minneapolis Skyline: Anthology of Minneapolis Poems*. Nan Fitz-Patrick, Ed. Minneapolis: The Colwell Press Inc., 1940, p. 71.

"Nests." *Poetry*, 24, May 1924, pp. 80-81.

"Poem for Elizabeth." *Mainstream*, 16, 5, May 1963, pp. 32-34.

"Spring Out of Jerusalem." *Scribners*, 93, April 1933, p. 234.

"The Dance of St. Paul, Then and Now and Yet." n.d. (1940's).

"Swing Low Sweet Valley," and others. *Minnesota Sings For Peace*. n.d.

"Walkers on a Frail Horizon." *From the Valley to the Mountains: Midwest Poetry*. Minneapolis: The Midwest Federation of Chaparral Poets Book Association, 1945, pp. 119-20.

"Run, Run, Come, Come," and others. *South Dakota Review*, 8, 3, Autumn, 1970, pp. 128-128.

Miscellaneous

"Letter to the Editor." *North Country Anvil*, 22, June-July 1977, p. 30.

"Join Hand and Brain." (book review) *World To Win* by Jack Conroy. *New Masses*, XVI, 2, July 9, 1934, p. 25.

"Heroes of China." (book review) *Daughters and Sons* by Kung Chueh and Yuan Ching. *Masses and Mainstream*, 5, 9, September 1952, pp. 58-60.

"Saga of the Steel Mills." (book review) *The Magic Fern* by Phillip Bonosky. *Mainstream*, 14, 10, October 1961, pp. 37-44.

"Notes on North Country Folkways." *Minnesota History*. 25, 3, September 1944, pp. 215-223.

"Let the Voice of the People Be Heard." Forward to *The Pavement Trail: A Collection of Poetry and Prose from the Allis-Chalmers Picket Lines*, June 1946.

"Where the Rain Falls: A Reverie — the Next Hundred Years." *The People Together*. Minneapolis: People's Centennial Book Committee of Minnesota, 1948, pp. 46-47.

"People Are the Story." *The People Together.* Minneapolis: People's
Centennial Book Committee of Minnesota, 1958, pp. 1-2.
"Journal Excerpts." *The Lamp In the Spine,* Summer/Fall 1974, pp.
94-126.
"Excerpts from 'The Origins of Corn.'" *New America: A Review,* 2, 3,
Summer-Fall 1976, pp. 20-23.
"Meridel Le Sueur." *Minnesota Writers.* Carmen Nelson Richards
and Genevieve Rose Breen, Eds. Minneapolis: Lund Press Inc.,
1945 (autobiographical)
"On a Drumhead." *Seventeen,* September 1947, p. 156 passim.
(autobiographical)
"The Ancient People and the Newly Come." *Growing Up in
Minnesota.* Chester G. Anderson, ed. Minneapolis: University of
Minnesota Press, 1976, pp. 17-46. (autobiographical)
"Tribute to Neruda," Tape with Tom McGrath, Robert Bly.
November 19, 1973, Minnesota Public Radio Audio Archive #A-
354, 60 min. (Le Sueur read from "Let the Rail Splitter Awake.")
"The Circle and the Square." Speech presented to Minneapolis
Unitarian Society, October 24, 1976, Tape.
"Struck to Ash Struck to Fire." *Great River Review,* 2, 1, 1979, pp.
31-46.

Selected Criticism, Reviews, and Interviews

Andrews, Jenne'. "Voice of Demeter," *Rites of Ancient Ripening.
Moons and Lion Tailes,* 11, 1, (1976), pp. 84-88.
Clausen, Jan. "The Girl," *Motheroot Journal* (Spring 1980): 3.
Clausen, Jan. "Review of *Women on the Breadlines, Harvest, Song for
My Time, Rites of Ancient Ripening,*" *Conditions: Three* (1978).
(Available from Box 56, Van Brunt Station, Brooklyn, N.Y.
11215).
"Continuous Woman." Film, 16mm, 30 min. Femme Films, Inc.
Gelfant, Blance. "Rereading a Radical." Review of *Ripening. The
New York Times Book Review,* April 4, 1982, pp. 7 passim.
Gorman, Katherine. St. Paul *Pioneer Press,* April 9, 1944.
Hale, Dorinda. "Le Sueur: Living, Writing from Within," *Sojourner*
3, 3 (Nov. 1977): 9, 21.
Hampl, Patricia, "Meridel Le Sueur — Voice of the Prairie," *MS.* 4, 2
(Aug. 1975): 62-6, 96.
"Interview," *West End Magazine* 5, 1 (Summer 1978): 8-14.

(Available from West End Press, Box 7232, Minneapolis, Minn. 55407)

Kirkpatrick, Patricia. "Meridel Le Sueur: In the Cycle of Root and Bloom." *Minnesota Daily*, November 19, 1973, pp. 9 passim.

"Le Sueur. Woman Writer, Political Activist," *Worker Writer* 1, 5: 1-2, 7.

"...on the far edge of the circle . . ." *Lady-Unique-Inclination-of-the-Night* (Autumn 1977): 14-15.

McAnally, Mary, ed., *We Sing Our Struggles: A Tribute To Us All For Meridel Le Sueur*. Tulsa, Oklahoma: Cardinal Press. 1982.

"Minnesota Rich in Material for Writing Says Author." Minneapolis *Morning Tribune*, October 6, 1947.

"My People Are My Home." Film, 16mm, 50 min. Produced by Femme Films, Inc., RR2, Box 28, Mankato, Minnesota 56001. Biographical, narrated by Le Sueur.

"New Book on Lincoln Has Pink Tinged Pages." rev. Milwaukee *Sentinel*, November 28, 1954.

Prokop, Kathee. "An Afternoon Shared with Meridel Le Sueur: Poet of People's History." *The Minnesota Leader*, VI, 5, February 10, 1975, p. 1 passim.

"Red Party Line Is Catch Line in New Abe Lincoln Book." Milwaukee *Sentinel*, November 28, 1954.

Review of *Ripening, Working Women*, September 1982, pp. 188-189.

[Schleuning]. Neala Yount, "America—Song We Sang Without Knowing—Meridel Le Sueur's America" (Ph.D. diss., University of Minnesota, 1978). (Pub. under Yount.)

Schleuning, Neala, J.Y. "Meridel Le Sueur: Toward a New Regionalism." *Books at Iowa*, 33 (November 1980), pp. 22-41.

Smith, Mara, "Meridel Le Sueur: A Bio-Bibliography" (Mimeographed, University of Minnesota, 1973).

Waterman, Charles. "Meridel Le Sueur: Forging Culture." *North Country Anvil* 22, June-July, 1977, pp. 22

Winegar, Karin. "Book Filters 82 years of Experience Into Clear Elixir," Review of *Ripening*, Minneapolis *Star and Tribune*, June 15, 1982, pp. 18 passim.